A Voice for Earth

EDITED BY PETER BLAZE CORCORAN
AND A. JAMES WOHLPART
Editorial Assistant Brandon P. Hollingshead

A Voice for Earth

American Writers Respond to the Earth Charter

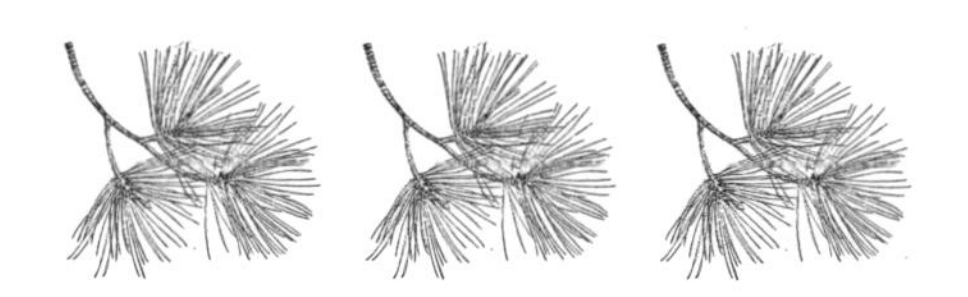

The University of Georgia Press
ATHENS AND LONDON

Acknowledgments for previously published works appear on page ix,
which constitutes an extension of the copyright page.

Athens, Georgia 30602

Based on design by Kathi Dailey Morgan
Set in 10.2 Electra by Newgen-Austin
Printed and bound by Thomson-Shore
The paper in this book meets the guidelines for
permanence and durability of the Committee on
Production Guidelines for Book Longevity of the
Council on Library Resources.
Printed in the United States of America
08 09 10 11 12 C 5 4 3 2 1
08 09 10 11 12 P 5 4 3 2 1
Library of Congress Cataloging-in-Publication Data
A voice for earth : American writers respond to the Earth Charter /
edited by Peter Blaze Corcoran and A. James Wohlpart ;
editorial assistant Brandon P. Hollingshead.
p. cm.
ISBN-13: 978-0-8203-3172-0 (hardcover : alk. paper)
ISBN-10: 0-8203-3172-4 (hardcover : alk. paper)
ISBN-13: 978-0-8203-3211-6 (pbk. : alk. paper)
ISBN-10: 0-8203-3211-9 (pbk. : alk. paper)
1. Earth Charter (1997). 2. Earth Charter (1997).
3. Human ecology. 4. Environmental protection.
I. Corcoran, Peter Blaze. II. Wohlpart, James, 1964–
GF47.V65 2008
333.72—dc22 2008014140
British Library Cataloging-in-Publication Data available

Publication of this book was made possible
in part by a subvention from the Office of the Provost
at Florida Gulf Coast University, the
FGCU Foundation, and FGCU's Center for Environmental
and Sustainability Education.

[W]e must decide to live with a sense of universal responsibility, identifying ourselves with the whole Earth community as well as our local communities. We are at once citizens of different nations and of one world in which the local and global are linked. Everyone shares responsibility for the present and future well-being of the human family and the larger living world. The spirit of human solidarity and kinship with all life is strengthened when we live with reverence for the mystery of being, gratitude for the gift of life, and humility regarding the human place in nature.

Earth Charter, Preamble, paragraph five

Contents

Acknowledgments *ix*

Foreword by Homero Aridjis,
The Rights of Nature *xi*

Foreword by Terry Tempest Williams,
Taking the Globe to Our Bosom *xiii*

Introduction *xix*
A. *James Wohlpart and Peter Blaze Corcoran*

Imagination into Principle

Crafting Principles for the Earth Charter 3
Steven C. Rockefeller

The Earth Charter 24

Principle into Imagination: Literary Responses to the Earth Charter

Owning the Imperatives: A Poem for the Earth Charter 37
Alison Hawthorne Deming

Learning to See the Stars: The Earth Charter as a Compass for the New Century 40
Mary Evelyn Tucker

Remembering the Ancient Path: The Original Instructions and the Earth Charter 54
Chief Jake Swamp

Lake Conestee 61
John Lane

Restoration: A Plan 68
Rick Bass

Wilderness as a Sabbath for the Land 80
Scott Russell Sanders

Who 90
Robert Michael Pyle

Broad Water, Distant Land 92
Stuart Ching

Possibility Begins Here 107
Lauret Savoy

Hope for Democracy 113
Janisse Ray

Imagination and Principle into a New Ethic

The Ethic of Care 129
Leonardo Boff, translated by Philip Berryman

Afterword 146
Kamla Chowdhry

Contributors 149

Acknowledgments

We thank the global people's movement that gave birth to the Earth Charter—the founding mothers and fathers, both well-known and unknown. The statement of widely shared global ethics that has come to inspire hope and action across the world is a passion for us and we acknowledge the great work of its creation.

We thank the contributors to this volume for their willingness to share their wisdom and for their patience with the long process of making this book. Their insights into the ethical nature of our situation at the start of the twenty-first century have moved us. We are honored to collect their work. We greatly appreciate the opportunity to include revised versions of two essays that had been previously published: Jake Swamp's "Remembering the Ancient Path: The Original Instructions and the Earth Charter" in *Faith Leaders on Intergroup Relations: Perspectives and Challenges* (National Conference on Community and Justice, 2002) and Scott Russell Sanders's "Wilderness as a Sabbath for the Land" in *Spiritus* (John Hopkins University Press, 2002).

We wish to acknowledge the profound support of Florida Gulf Coast University through this process. The administration has embraced our Earth Charter scholarship and encouraged our research through the University's Center for Environmental and Sustainability Education, which we direct. The Center enjoys broad administrative support, which we treasure. Special thanks to the Dean of the College of Arts and Sciences Donna Price Henry, former Provost and Vice President for Academic Affairs Bonnie Yegidis, Vice President for Administrative Services and Finance Joe Shepard, and Vice President for University Advancement Steve Magiera.

Our work at the Center is made possible by our able student assistants. We wish to acknowledge the mature editorial assistance of

Brandon P. Hollingshead on this project, the good-humored organizational assistance of Jessica Solimano, and the earnest initiative of Joseph Weakland. We thank Florida Gulf Coast University faculty and staff who contribute to the Center as Associates. We also thank our distinguished Board of Advisors, co-chaired by David Orr and Mary Evelyn Tucker, who inspire us by their commitment to Earth—and to the Earth Charter.

Foreword by Homero Aridjis

The Rights of Nature

At this critical moment in the natural history of Earth, two hundred and nineteen years after the Declaration of the Rights of Man (1789) was adopted in revolutionary France and sixty years after the United Nations proclaimed the Universal Declaration of Human Rights (1948), it is time for the world community to embrace a global covenant that sets forth the fundamental Rights of Nature.

We might wonder how countries that have yet to recognize officially or to honor fully human rights can be expected to respect the Rights of Nature. Yet the struggle for the safekeeping and survival of thousands of animal and plant species is an integral part of the struggle for the safekeeping and survival of the human race. An environmentally degraded planet degrades humankind because our physical and spiritual welfare depends on the health of our natural environment.

Since the origins of life, and as evolution progressed, the destiny of human beings and the rise of nature have been inextricably linked. Nature can survive without humans, but humans cannot survive without nature. The vertiginous disappearance of species from the face of the planet is unprecedented in history and points the way toward our own extinction. It is not enough to preserve a select fraction of the world's flora and fauna in zoos and botanical gardens; all species must be kept alive in the places where they are born, thrive, and reproduce. Their *oikos*, their habitat, must be their sanctuary. From a divine or a natural point of view, an animal or plant species is no individual's property, nor is a species the property of any particular country; no person or group has the right to lay down conditions which limit a species' right to life. Each is a creature of Earth and is entitled to reside on it with dignity.

The world has room enough for all existing life-forms, but every day humans increase in number and claim more space to satisfy their needs and greed. To get what we want, humans raze temperate conifer forests and tropical rainforests; pollute and depredate rivers, lakes, and oceans; poison the soil and wreak havoc on wetlands, coral reefs, and deserts—indiscriminately destroying the habitats of whatever walks, swims, flies, crawls, or grows. This relentless encroachment on the natural world must be seen as negative development, as humanity's march toward death. And it must be stopped.

The excessive enrichment of a small number of individuals or groups impoverishes us all. Earth must not become a silent, sterile desert, the dark garden of our worst imaginings. It is up to humans, who are rational animals with a moral conscience, to defend the right to exist of other creatures, and of plants—and not to be their executioners.

The Greek Stoics believed that man was connected with the Universe and was meant to play a part in it. They saw the Universe as a living organism with a soul, the embodiment of deity. That deity was the universal Law of Nature. The individual *logos*, the principle of rationality, was the universal Logos of Nature. Today more than ever, humans must perceive losses in nature as our own personal losses. We must reflect on the denaturalized life that threatens to be ours, for we are an organic part of the natural world.

Sixteen years after the first global summit for the environment in Rio de Janeiro (1992), and eight years into the third millennium, we must cherish the living masterpieces of nature, because as Parmenides said, "All is full of Being." The Earth Charter provides us with an ethical framework for recognizing the Rights of Nature that will allow us to live a sustainable existence. The rights of humans for social justice, nonviolence, and democracy have been widely recognized; in this way the unique contribution of the Earth Charter is to demonstrate the interconnectedness of human rights and the Rights of Nature. *A Voice for Earth: American Writers Respond to the Earth Charter* provides a new way of being and thinking founded on the integrated ethical principles of this covenant that is especially important to consider in North America.

Foreword by Terry Tempest Williams

Taking the Globe to Our Bosom

The United Nations is an ideal, and it remains so. Its charter articulates its vision "to practice tolerance and live together in peace with one another as good neighbors, and to unite our strength to maintain international peace and security." Each time I enter its hallowed space designed for dialogue and shared power, I find my wearied hope revived. Especially in times of war, the rigidity of nationalism becomes the embrace of humanity. Possibility replaces inevitability.

In this same way, the Earth Charter is an ideal. It is a visionary document that creates a template for ecological consciousness around the world, rooted in local actions. It asks us to embrace the planet while taking care of our own backyards.

I like thinking this small and this large.

In 1946, E. B. White wrote that "the focus of our alliance will have to shift or we will find ourselves at last with nothing left to be loyal to. A world government, were we ever to get one, would impose on the individual the curious burden of taking the entire globe to his bosom—although not in any sense depriving him of the love of his front yard."

There is nothing wrong with sweeping gestures or communal dreams brought to life through the struggle of looking into another's eyes and asking the question, "What do we do?" Indeed, our alliances shift as our frame of reference widens. The United Nations was born after two world wars. The Earth Charter was conceived in preparation for the Earth Summit in Rio in 1992. Climate change was already on the minds of scientists and humanitarians around the globe. It is in such bold moments of unwavering love and need that social reform is born.

Consider the United States Constitution and the United Nations Universal Declaration of Human Rights. These are two documents of desire that demand a different world from us, a world made accountable, a world where human dignity is the white-hot center of justice and freedom. We know these great manifestos indicate not the end of transformative thought, but a beginning of creative collaborations. And they are never to be taken for granted. Despots and tyrants will always try to take more power for themselves, but an enlivened citizenry can ensure that these documents' intentions will be safeguarded and realized. The Earth Charter, called "an ethical lodestar" by Pakistan's Parvez Hassan, belongs to this family of compassionate and illuminated thinking.

We know in our bones that the world is broken. We know in our hearts that we are all complicit in our addiction to oil: we drive, we fly, we heat our homes. At whose expense? Governments and corporations around the world are fostering the old patterns that promote and profit from a consumptive model of growth. Who benefits?

We know in the fullness of our being that the lives we are living are not sustainable. Someone is paying the price.

"We stand at a critical moment in Earth's history, a time when humanity must choose its future."[1] The first sentence of the Preamble of the Earth Charter is central to our awareness, understanding, and evolution as a species. We can no longer afford to live in denial of our role in the fracturing and fragmentation of the planet. We can begin to build a new ethical structure globally founded on empathy, not economics, a framework based on giving, not taking, and on a model of cooperation, not competition. A different kind of education is necessary, one that courts creativity from time spent in nature, not an education committed to test scores and rote memorization of facts and figures. The "great work" of creating a planetary culture of care based on holistic thinking, not reductive discourse, is inherent in the expansive web of the arts, humanities, and sciences. This is the "dream of the Earth" that the theologian Thomas Berry has outlined.

I have always held fast to these words of Nobel Peace Prize activist Aung San Suu Kyi: "It is our attempt to engage in the struggle that matters. The struggle itself is the most important thing." The Earth Charter is an acknowledgment of our struggle to live in harmony with Earth, as well as an attempt to weave together Respect and Care for the Community of Life, Ecological Integrity, Social and Economic Justice, and Democracy, Nonviolence, and Peace into a cohesive embrace of behavior toward all life.

Steven C. Rockefeller, one of the chief architects of the Earth Charter, writes: "The Earth Charter focuses attention on the need for global ethics. It is concerned with the identification and promotion of ethical values that are widely shared in all nations, cultures, and religions—what some philosophers call universal values. Global ethics are of critical importance in the Great Transition because we live in an increasingly interdependent, fragile, and complex world . . . global interdependence means that no community or nation can mange its problems by itself. Partnership and collaboration are essential."

Mary Evelyn Tucker, another intellectual pillar of the Earth Charter, writes, "Indeed, the twenty-first century may be remembered as the century in which humans laid the foundations for the well-being of the planet as a whole by embracing the Earth Community."

And this from the Preamble: "To move forward we must recognize that in the midst of a magnificent diversity of cultures and life forms we are one human family and one Earth community with a common destiny."[2]

I love these words and I believe them. They lead us naturally to what Aldo Leopold outlines in "The Land Ethic" from *A Sand County Almanac*, that we belong to a community that includes all life forms: plants, animals, and human beings.

Empathy comes to mind. We are at our highest evolutionary state of being when we exercise respect and regard toward another. To feel with others, to imagine where they stand and from where they speak, this too, becomes "our common destiny." Do we dare to acknowledge the word "love"? This soul-transference of care and understanding can also be extended beyond our own species.

Last winter in Jackson Hole, Wyoming, a story circulated from neighbor to neighbor, from household to household. It had been wickedly cold, six weeks of subzero temperatures, so bitter that when you were outside your lungs ached with each breath and your teeth felt as though they might shatter. For the most part, people stayed inside.

But one man did not. He was out cross-country skiing in a meadow near his home. It was snowing. Through the flurries, he saw a baby moose on one side of a barbed wire fence; its mother was standing on the other side. The baby was bawling. The mother was agitated, raising her head up and down.

As the man got a bit closer and his eyes cleared from the cold, he could see that one of the young moose's spindly legs was caught in the barbed wire that was now twisted around it.

The man quietly moved closer to the two moose on his skis, all the while speaking to them in a low, calm, comforting voice, "You're okay, little one. I'm so sorry—I'm going to try and get that barbed wire off of you." And then turning to the cow moose, he said, "I know you're not going to like this, but I need you to let me help your baby untangle his leg—I need you to trust me and then I'll be on my way. I mean you no harm."

The female moose just stood still. Her ears remained forward, not pulled back as a sign of aggression.

"That's it, little one—I'm here to help—one minute—just give me one minute." And in about that time or less, this good Samaritan on skis quickly leaned forward, untangled the barbed wire from around the baby's leg and helped him find his way to the side where its mother was waiting—and then went on his way.

Does it matter if the moose understood what the man was saying to her? What mattered is that she allowed the human intervention on behalf of her calf. Something was transmitted species to species, something was understood and a life was spared from pain.

I like to think of the Earth Charter as a calm conversation in the name of a caring and compassionate community. I like to think of the Earth Charter as a whisper in the ear of one who is ill, not offering a prescription of a pill or an invasive operation, but rather the gentle admonition of a friend who says, "Breathe—Take my hand, we will find a way through this, together."

When Aldo Leopold spoke of "land health" I believe this is what he had in mind.

I like to think of the Earth Charter as a promise to our planet. *We will be present with you. We will not turn our backs on the poverty of our brothers and sisters. We will not walk away from our commitment to face whatever the future may bring. We will watch, listen, speak, and act on behalf of "a reverence for life."*

Albert Schweitzer pared his lifelong philosophical and religious pursuits down to these three words, "reverence for life." The Earth Charter revives this compelling thought and puts it into a working plan of action.

The editors and contributors to this vibrant collection are friends. Peter Blaze Corcoran and Jim Wohlpart are heroes of mine. They are not only champions of freedom of speech; they are fearless in their love for the land and all its inhabitants. Their collective work at Florida Gulf Coast University through the Center for Environmental and Sustainability Education is creating the next generation of scholars and activists through their own examples and devotion to emancipatory education. The Earth Charter has been and continues to be a blueprint for the future they are nurturing.

The American writers in this collection from Rick Bass in the Northern Rockies to Alison Hawthorne Deming in the Sonoran Desert to Robert Michael Pyle in the Pacific Northwest to Lauret Savoy in the Northeast to Janisse Ray in the American South are all writers deeply connected to place and the furthering of this ethical stance toward life. That they would embrace the Earth Charter as an extension of their own writing and citizenship makes perfect sense if one follows their own evolutionary thinking; local care is planetary care.

Steven C. Rockefeller, Mary Evelyn Tucker, Chief Jake Swamp, and Homero Aridjis can be considered elders among us.

Each essay in *A Voice for Earth* becomes a bow to a world where "justice for all" means justice for the voiceless, human and wild. It is a collective call for a change of heart that will carry us forward, even in this uncertain world where clouds are gathering.

Too many of us in the United States of America doubt the reality of a warming planet. Too many of us in this country live both extravagant and expedient lives without a thought about those who carry the debts of our lifestyles. We are all complicit. And too many of us are too comfortable to care about those who are not.

It is my great hope that we as Americans can begin to understand a "sacrifice" not as something we must give up, but rather as an offering made on behalf of another. Sacrifice becomes a gesture of love, not loss. I believe we have this kind of generosity of spirit. I believe this is what the writers in this collection are asking us to consider as we come to a greater understanding of what the Earth Charter is and why it is so necessary as both an ideal and an implement in this time of transition.

May we find and hold the last sentence in the Earth Charter from "The Way Forward" as a beacon of light in this beautiful, broken world: "Let ours be a time remembered for the awakening of a new reverence for life, the firm resolve to achieve sustainability, the quickening of the struggle for justice and peace, and the joyful celebration of life."[3]

NOTES

1. Earth Charter, Preamble, paragraph one.
2. Ibid.
3. Earth Charter, The Way Forward, paragraph five.

Introduction

A. James Wohlpart and Peter Blaze Corcoran

> As never before in history, common destiny beckons us to seek a new beginning. Such renewal is the promise of these Earth Charter principles. To fulfill this promise, we must commit ourselves to adopt and promote the values and objectives of the Charter.
>
> This requires a change of mind and heart. It requires a new sense of global interdependence and universal responsibility. We must imaginatively develop and apply the vision of a sustainable way of life locally, nationally, regionally, and globally. Our cultural diversity is a precious heritage and different cultures will find their own distinctive ways to realize the vision. We must deepen and expand the global dialogue that generated the Earth Charter, for we have much to learn from the ongoing collaborative search for truth and wisdom.
>
> from the Earth Charter, The Way Forward

Twenty years ago a call was issued for "new norms for state and interstate behaviour needed to maintain livelihoods and life on our shared planet."[1] The World Commission on Environment and Development (WCED), chaired by Gro Harlem Brundtland, wrote in its classic *Our Common Future*, "there is now a need to consolidate and extend relevant legal principles in a new charter to guide state behaviour in the transition to sustainable development."[2] The WCED was convinced "that the security, well-being, and very survival of the planet depend on such changes, now."[3] In the lead-up to the

1992 Rio United Nations Conference on Environment and Development (UNCED), both national governments and nongovernmental organizations demonstrated considerable enthusiasm for such a charter that would embody and even reach beyond existing agreements and conventions for sustainable development. The hope of a new charter was that it would provide an ethical foundation upon which the UNCED agreements could be based.

While much good resulted from the Rio Earth Summit, as it came to be called, such a charter did not. Yet, because of the Summit, some governments and many nongovernmental organizations came to recognize the paramount importance of creating a document that outlined common principles for interacting in the increasingly interconnected world. In addition, the Rio Earth Summit provided a foundation for the emergence of a participatory worldwide process of building consensus on shared ethical values. According to Mirian Vilela, longtime Executive Director of the Earth Charter Initiative, the 1992 Rio Earth Summit, the end of the Cold War, and the progress of communication technology were key elements that marked the beginning of a new era in the development of such a global document.[4]

The failure in intergovernmental negotiations to draft a new charter at the 1992 Rio Earth Summit allowed for the emergence of broader involvement of civil society in this project. Significantly, the shift from governmental control to civil society involvement also enabled the drafting process to benefit from diverse input from the international community and from various conceptual agreements reached at the UN summits held over the decade of the 1990s.[5] In 1994, after nongovernmental members from nineteen countries developed an initial draft that was based on work completed at the Rio Earth Summit, the creation of an "Earth Charter," as it had come to be known, shifted fully to a civil society project under the leadership of Maurice F. Strong, who had chaired the Rio conference and was Chair of the Earth Council, and Mikhail Gorbachev, who was President of Green Cross International.

From 1994 to 2000, extensive research, consultation, and drafting took place throughout the world. To the best of our knowledge, the Earth Charter Initiative has involved the most open and participatory consultation process ever conducted in connection with the drafting of an international document. Tens of thousands of individuals and hundreds of organizations from all regions of the world, from different cultures, and from diverse sectors of society participated. The Charter was shaped by experts, government and civil society leaders, students, and representatives from indigenous groups and grassroots communities.[6] In late 1996, the Earth Council and Maurice F. Strong, in consultation with Mikhail Gorbachev, formed an Earth Charter Commission—a distinguished group of leaders from many sectors, cultures, and regions of the world.[7] The first meeting of the Commission occurred in March 1997 during the Rio+5 Forum (a UN forum five years after the 1992 Rio Earth Summit). Just after the formation of the Commission in December 1996, Steven C. Rockefeller was asked to chair and form a Drafting Committee; he had been coordinating research on the Earth Charter Principles. In March 2000, the Earth Charter Commission officially adopted the Earth Charter in Paris and it was launched at the Peace Palace in The Hague three months later.

The story of the creation of the Earth Charter is dramatic and inspiring. In some ways, the most amazing thing about the Earth Charter is that it exists at all, given the challenges of working across the many divides that characterize the postmodern world—Northern and Southern hemispheres, faith traditions, political perspectives, and generations.

Once launched, a new phase in the life of the Earth Charter began, which involved circulation and endorsement of the document as a grassroots treaty to advance a sustainable future. The major objectives of the Earth Charter movement were to promote a worldwide dialogue on shared values and global ethics; to set forth a succinct and inspiring vision of fundamental ethical principles for sustainable development; to circulate the Earth Charter throughout the world as a people's treaty, promoting awareness, commitment, and implementation of Earth Charter values; and to seek endorsement of the Earth Charter by the United Nations General Assembly. Since 2000, the existence and value of the Earth Charter have been celebrated in many countries across the world by those in many fields of endeavor—youth activism, international law, social and environmental justice, women's issues, poverty alleviation, diplomacy, education, business, animal rights, and many more. However, in those first five years of the Earth Charter, two critical needs of the Earth Charter movement emerged: the need to demonstrate and document the efficacy of the Earth Charter across many fields and types of problems and the need to express the meaning of the Earth Charter Principles in ways that help people to understand their significance and inspire them to action.

The first of these needs was met with the launch of *The Earth Charter in Action: Toward a Sustainable World* at the Earth Charter+5 meeting in Amsterdam in November 2005 held five years after the completion of the Earth Charter.[8] *The Earth Charter in Action* describes the ways in which the Earth Charter has been used in such activities as revising educational systems, negotiating social constructs, and mitigating environmental damage. Thematic and descriptive essays and artwork from around the world demonstrate its utility in diverse cultural contexts. They show its promise in working across the divide between the Northern and Southern hemispheres, across the faith traditions, the nations, and the generations.

The second of these needs has, until now, remained unmet. The meaning of the Earth Charter, in spite of its comprehensive nature and compelling language, is somewhat difficult to access. *A Voice for Earth: American Writers Respond to the Earth Charter* offers a literary language that seeks to bring to life the concepts in the Earth Charter. We trust that these works do so with a richness of interpretation and possibility, though not in an authoritative way, but rather in a way that allows translation into different cultural settings. The works collected here demonstrate, through the vitality of literature, the power and importance of the ethical principles of the Earth Charter. The contributions are intended to awaken an understanding of the ethical nature of our current situation and to offer a rich and fertile rendering of the ways in which ethical principles connect our daily lives to wider political, economic, and social concerns.

We believe that this awakened understanding is especially important for citizens of the United States of America. The heart of *A Voice for Earth*, titled "Principle into Imagination," contains essays, poems, and stories by writers from the United States who reflect on a wide variety of principles in the Earth Charter. The two primary goals of these works are to introduce North Americans to the Earth Charter and to open a dialogue concerning the ethical implications of our current situation. Because many in the United States are not familiar with the Earth Charter, the central part focuses on voices from America that open a pathway into the Earth Charter. The second foreword, by Terry Tempest Williams, a noted activist and writer from the United States, invites the reader down this path. However, because the Earth Charter has great currency outside of the United States, the first foreword, the concluding essay in the part "Imagination and Principle into a New Ethic," and the afterword are by writers who have worked deeply with the Earth Charter in their own countries. Homero Aridjis, Leonardo Boff, and the late Kamla Chowdhry played significant roles in the conception of the intellectual architecture of the Earth Charter and in its coming-into-being. Nevertheless, the core of the book is by writers from the United States who, we believe, are especially well qualified to bring the integrated ethical vision of the Earth Charter to our country, where it is so much needed.

In the introductory part of *A Voice for Earth*, "Imagination into Principle," Steven C. Rockefeller, the Chair of the Earth Charter Drafting Committee, and an American, describes the process that governed the writing of the document and provides several poignant examples of how complex issues and problems in selecting specific language and dealing with particular concepts were addressed. His essay, "Crafting Principles for the Earth Charter," highlights the way in which a wide range of input was used to distill complex ideas into succinct ethical statements that are consistent with the worldviews of the many constituents involved in the drafting process. The writing of the Earth Charter—the selection of particular words, the emphasis on particular ethical concepts, the arrangement of particular ideas—provides an example of humans' ability to speak across cultures and, more importantly, to listen, to compromise, and to come to consensus.

The main part of *A Voice for Earth*, "Principle into Imagination," opens with Alison Hawthorne Deming's "Owning the Imperatives: A Poem for the Earth Charter," which offers a literary rendition of each of the sixteen principles of the Earth Charter. Deming passes each principle through her poetic imagination and transforms the rather universal Earth Charter language into actions that speak to individuals. For instance, Principle 9, "Eradicate poverty as an ethical, social, and environmental imperative" becomes "Eradicate the desperation of the poor by swapping anger, alleyways and ashcans for books, bicycles and bags of wheat." In this poetic alchemy, Deming gives voice to what lies behind the Earth Charter principle and connects it to the reader's imagination; the "poverty" to be eradicated is transformed into the "desperation of the poor," and the "ethical, social, and environmental imperative" becomes "books, bicycles and bags of wheat," significantly more concrete concepts that the reader can grasp. "Owning the Imperatives" thus turns Earth Charter principles into concrete actions that can be taken by individuals.

The two works that follow Deming's poem, Mary Evelyn Tucker's "Learning to See the Stars: The Earth Charter as a Compass for the New Century" and Chief Jake Swamp's "Remembering the Ancient Path: The Original Instructions and the Earth Charter," reflect on the way in which our contemporary societies have lost their way and offer hope in the idea of recapturing the wisdom of ancient ways. Tucker's essay uses the Hokulea voyages that re-created the ancestral Hawaiian voyages to the South Pacific islands as a frame for discussing her own intellectual journey. Through reconnecting with ancient navigation techniques, through relearning how to read the stars, the moon, the sun, the waves, the narrator of this story journeys back in time and relearns a knowledge not offered through modern-day science. In the essay, Tucker charts her own personal journey through diverse and ancient cultures to a new perspective, one based on respect for individual cultural and ethical values balanced with an awareness of the need to create a shared, sustainable future. Likewise, Chief Jake Swamp's essay, "Remembering the Ancient Path," reflects on the way in which even his native culture of the Haudenosaunee has become disconnected from the beliefs that once guided them in their relationship to the universe. Through comparing the beliefs of the "Original Instructions" to the principles in the Earth Charter, Swamp suggests that we might engender a dialogue that will allow all cultures to again respect the sacredness of the universe that sustains us. Such a dialogue is central to the Earth Charter, which seeks to broaden our ethical vision to include the wider community of life and the interdependent relationships that exist in that community.

The next three works, John Lane's "Lake Conestee," Rick Bass's "Restoration: A Plan," and Scott Russell Sanders's "Wilderness as a Sabbath for the Land," focus on the relationship between humans and the land, describing the destructiveness of that relationship while also suggesting ways for us to create a new, sustainable relationship. The essays by Lane and Bass focus on revealing the harm that humans have wreaked on Earth through describing the impact of textile mills in the southern United States and the havoc inflicted on wilderness by the logging industry in the western United States. Yet these essays also provide hope by calling for a new vision and a new story; they offer an alternative relation to the historical relation to the land, which has viewed rivers and lakes as places to dump industrial wastes and forests as places to harvest timber without considering the wider ecological systems that are ruined, not to mention the loss of wildness that ensues. The last essay also offers a hopeful vision by arguing for an expanded view of our ethical responsibilities that takes into account the rights of the wider community of life that sustains us. Sanders draws a parallel between preserving the seventh day of the week, the sabbath, as a holy day of rest and preserving a small portion of the wilderness as a place untouched by human dominion, for, he argues, "the wilderness represents in space what the sabbath represents in time." All three of these essays, founded on key principles of the Earth Charter that deal with sustainability and ecological integrity, extend the ethical imperatives that guide our lives through forcing us to engage a broader vision of the responsibilities of humans and of the rights of the other-than-human.

The next four works—Robert Michael Pyle's "Who," Stuart Ching's "Broad Water, Distant Land," Lauret Savoy's "Possibility Begins Here," and Janisse Ray's "Hope for Democracy"—focus on issues of social, economic, and political justice, revealing the way in which we need a cultural shift, one based on the values outlined in the Earth Charter. Pyle's poem recounts the devastation that humans have brought to Earth and the resulting global instability;

Pyle ultimately calls to question a fundamental issue in the Earth Charter: who will be responsible for caring and honoring and acting on these new ethical principles? Ching's short story brings issues of social and economic disenfranchisement to life through describing the desecration of land that occurs as a result of modern-day development. Ching depicts the confusion and conflict that occurs in the clash of worldviews through unfolding the complex relationship between two boys, one who descends from native Hawaiians and one who descends from Japanese immigrants. Like Ching, Savoy connects issues of social justice to issues of environmental degradation; through telling her own story of the struggle with her identity as a "mixedblood" person, she connects the historical disenfranchisement of large sectors of the human family to the compromising of the integrity of the landscape. In the last essay in "Principle into Imagination," "Hope for Democracy," Ray brings the larger questions of political disenfranchisement raised in Savoy's essay to bear on our contemporary political scene. She recounts her own frustration at what she sees as the weakening of democratic institutions in the United States and refers to the Earth Charter as a means to rectify this situation.

In the concluding part of *A Voice for Earth*, "Imagination and Principle into a New Ethic," Leonardo Boff offers in "The Ethic of Care" a new paradigm for right living created from reflecting on the concept of care as it is embodied in the Earth Charter. Boff offers an historical basis for his reflection on care, referring to the Greek fable that suggests "care" is the true essence of human beings and to the cosmological and biological fact that the universe and life itself would not exist without care. Ultimately, Boff suggests that care can provide a foundation for a new way of being in this time of crisis that can lead us from the path of self-destruction toward a path of "universal coresponsibility." Through care, we can redirect our social, economic, and political actions toward a path of sustainability. Because humans and Earth that sustains us comprise one interconnected system, we must urgently reformulate our ethical principles to be founded on the concept of care as the Earth Charter suggests.

As the counterpart to Rockefeller's historical introduction, which focuses on the crafting of the Earth Charter principles, Boff's forward-looking and philosophical conclusion offers a reformulation of the ethical principles under what he calls the "sign of care." The essays bookended by these two parts of *A Voice for Earth*, those in the main section titled "Principle into Imagination," are all by authors from the United States responding to the Earth Charter through their own creative pathways. These American voices are critical because the United States must begin to accept the ethical responsibility for its overconsumption and creation of an unsustainable future. The writers included in this book have read the Earth Charter deeply and offer their own creative responses to the ethical principles embodied in the document in hopes of inspiring a shift in our culture.

Like the writers in this book, in the days before the World Summit on Sustainable Development in Johannesburg, South Africa, in 2002, the youth of nearby Diepsloot responded to the Earth Charter through writing, singing, and dancing. By day they studied and discussed the Earth Charter and invited the meaning of its ethical principles to inspire their creativity and imagination. By night they slept on the dusty earth of Diepsloot, an informal settlement near Johannesburg, encircling and protecting the Ark of Hope that had journeyed to them from the United Nations in New York City.

The Ark of Hope, a handmade wooden vessel weighing over a thousand kilograms with the words of the Earth Charter hand-scripted on papyrus inside its lid, carries dozens of Temenos Books inside. These are small hand-crafted books with pictures and poems and words that capture responses to the Earth Charter from across generations, backgrounds, nations, and faith traditions. Sally Linder and Cameron Davis, creators of the project, have written,

> Together, the Ark of Hope and Temenos Books have awakened more than ten thousand people around the world to the promise of the Charter, warming their hearts to its principles and energizing their imaginations with its tremendous potential. . . . From our experience, we knew that art has the capacity to engage inner dialogue with the external issues of the world. . . . Deepest desires and dreams are embodied in each Temenos Book.[9]

The gathering together of these books crafted from across the world is itself an act of hope that attests to humans' abiding belief in the power of art to transform our world.

The singing and dancing and talking of the youth of Diepsloot grew in the days leading up to the World Summit and manifested in the creation of their own Temenos Books. Thus were the aspirations and worries of Diepsloot youth joined with those of others across the world. Like many others, theirs is a community of extreme poverty and difficulty, including unemployment and HIV infection rates running as high as eighty percent among the young. On the first day of the World Summit, these young women and men carried the Ark of Hope through the streets of Johannesburg and presented it to the hundreds of world leaders gathered to seek the path to a sustainable future.

The capturing of the responses of the young people of Diepsloot to the Earth Charter is analogous to our goal in this volume. The hope of *A Voice for Earth* is to articulate a new story built upon a new way of being in the world. As many of the works suggest, this new way of being will be founded on an enlarged worldview that takes into account future human generations along with the other-than-human. Several of the pieces in the collection describe how we have lost our way, how we have lost a sense of values that could guide us down a path that is sustainable not only in our relationship to Earth but also to spirit. Yet these literary responses also lay the groundwork for charting a new path, for recapturing the wisdom of ancient traditions and reformulating current practices and beliefs. The new story of the twenty-first century as envisioned in these works can lead us to a world of ecological integrity and nonviolence, a world that protects life on Earth and is founded on sustainable economic, political, and social systems, a world that sustains not only our physical bodies but also our spirits.

NOTES

1. World Commission on Environment and Development, *Our Common Future* (Oxford: Oxford University Press, 1987), 332.

2. Ibid. The full quote reads: "Building on the 1972 Declaration, the 1982 Nairobi Declaration, and many existing international conventions and General Assembly resolutions, there is now a need to consolidate and extend relevant legal principles in a new charter to guide state behaviour in the transition to

sustainable development. It would provide the basis for, and be subsequently expanded into, a Convention, setting out the sovereign rights and reciprocal responsibilities of all states on environmental protection and sustainable development. The charter should prescribe new norms for state and interstate behaviour needed to maintain livelihoods and life on our shared planet, including basic norms for prior notification, consultation, and assessment of activities likely to have an impact on neighboring states or global commons."

3. Ibid., 343.

4. Vilela now serves as Executive Director of the Earth Charter Initiative. She plays a vital role in the successful realization of the Earth Charter.

5. Mirian Vilela and Peter Blaze Corcoran, "Building Consensus on Shared Values." In Peter Blaze Corcoran, ed., *The Earth Charter in Action: Toward a Sustainable World* (Amsterdam: Royal Tropical Institute [KIT] Publishers, 2005), 18.

6. Our account of the early history of the Earth Charter relies on the writing of others, primarily Steven C. Rockefeller, Chair of the drafting committee, to whom we are indebted for his insight.

7. The Earth Charter Commission members were selected from different areas of the world in order to include a full representation of voices and perspectives.

AFRICA AND THE MIDDLE EAST
Amadou Toumani Tore, Mali
Princess Basma Bint Talal, Jordan
Wangari Maathai, Kenya
Mohamed Sahnoun, Algeria

ASIA AND THE PACIFIC
Kamla Chowdhry, India
A. T. Ariyaratne, Sri Lanka
Wakako Hironaka, Japan
Pauline Tangiora, New Zealand/Aotearoa
Erna Witolear, Indonesia

EUROPE
Mikhail Gorbachev, Russia
Pierre Calame, France
Ruud Lubbers, The Netherlands
Federico Mayor, Spain
Henriette Rassmussen, Greenland
Awraham Soetendorp, The Netherlands

NORTH AMERICA
Maurice F. Strong, Canada
John Hoyt, United States of America
Elizabeth May, Canada
Steven C. Rockefeller, United States of America
Severn Cullis-Suzuki, Canada

LATIN AMERICA AND THE CARIBBEAN
Mercedes Sosa, Argentina
Leonardo Boff, Brazil
Yolanda Kakabadse, Ecuador
Shridath Ramphal, Guyana

8. Corcoran, *The Earth Charter in Action*. Available online at <http://earth-charterinaction.org/eci_book.html>.

9. Sally Linder and Cameron Davis, "The Ark of Hope and the Temenos Books." In Corcoran, *The Earth Charter in Action*, 147.

Imagination into Principle

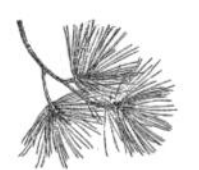

Crafting Principles for the Earth Charter

Steven C. Rockefeller

The Earth Charter, completed and launched in 2000, is a declaration of fundamental principles for building a just, sustainable, and peaceful world. It is the product of a ten-year, worldwide, cross-cultural dialogue on common goals and shared values. The objective of the consultation and drafting process was to help crystallize and articulate the consensus on shared values related to sustainable development taking form in the emerging global civil society. This essay endeavors to describe the Earth Charter consultation and drafting process and presents examples of how controversial issues and complex problems were addressed. Some issues were resolved quickly, and others required discussions that continued for over two years. Many individuals representing diverse constituencies and points of view played critical roles in the dialogue process. In this essay, it is possible to cite only a few selected examples of these important contributions.

In *Our Common Future* (1987), the report of the World Commission on Environment and Development, a recommendation is made to create "a new charter to guide state behaviour in the transition to sustainable development."[1] Convinced of the urgent need for a new international agreement of this nature, Maurice Strong, acting in his capacity as Secretary-General of the 1992 United Nations Conference on Environment and Development (UNCED), endeavored to interest governments in drafting an "Earth Charter." During the preparatory process for UNCED, a number of governments and civil society organizations submitted recommendations for the proposed Earth Charter. However, there was not sufficient government support, and the idea of drafting the Earth Charter as an intergovernmental document had to be abandoned. Following UNCED, Maurice Strong created the Earth Council to promote the transition to sustainable development, and in 1994, as chair of the Earth Council, he joined with Mikhail Gorbachev, the president of Green Cross International, to launch a civil society initiative to draft the Earth Charter as a people's charter.

The Earth Charter Initiative was based at the Earth Council in Costa Rica, and Ambassador Mohamed Sahnoun of Algeria became the first executive director of the project. From the start, it was recognized that a worldwide Earth Charter consultation process would be in itself a highly significant educational undertaking in support of global ethics and that the future authority of the Earth Charter would depend on conducting the most inclusive and participatory process ever associated with the drafting of an international declaration. For these reasons the process was considered to be as important as the final product.

New international consultations on what should be included in the Earth Charter began in 1995.[2] At the same time, extensive research was conducted in the fields of international environmental and sustainable development law, environmental science, philosophy, religion, and ethics.[3] In December 1996 the Earth Council and Green Cross International formed an Earth Charter Commission to oversee the drafting process. The Commission had twenty-three members with representatives from Africa, the Middle East, Asia and the Pacific, Europe, Latin America and the Caribbean, and North America. Early in 1997, an international drafting committee was formed, and it worked closely with the Earth Council, which was headed by Maximo Kalaw of the Philippines. During the drafting process Mirian Vilela of Brazil served as the Earth Charter coordinator at the Earth Council.[4]

Early in the process, the Commission and drafting committee developed a general concept for the Charter. It was agreed that the document should be:

- A declaration of fundamental ethical principles for environmental conservation and a sustainable way of life.
- A statement of principles of enduring significance that are widely shared by people of all cultures, religions, and races.
- A relatively brief and concise document composed in a language that is inspiring, clear, and uniquely valid and meaningful in all languages.
- A document with a holistic perspective that includes articulation of universal spiritual values as well as ethical principles.
- A call to action that adds significant new dimensions of value to what has been expressed in UN declarations and other relevant documents.
- A people's treaty that serves as a universal code of conduct for civil society, business, and national councils of sustainable development.
- A declaration of principles that establishes norms and aspirations for the behavior of state governments and that can serve as a soft law document if endorsement by the UN General Assembly is secured.[5]

In order to keep the Charter a relatively short document, it was agreed that the Charter should be limited to fundamental principles and very general strategic guidelines. Consequently, the document does not discuss the mechanisms and instruments required to implement its principles. The Commission also recognized that different cultures and communities will adopt their own distinctive approaches to the implementation of Earth Charter goals and values.

The drafting committee was well aware that diverse groups might have very different philosophical or religious reasons for supporting certain shared ethical values. In this regard, what was important was that people could reach ethical agreement in spite of significant cultural and intellectual differences. The committee respected these differences and was not concerned with trying to bridge them. Critics of global ethics initiatives often argue that promoters of universal values inevitably engage in some form of cultural imperialism.

However, the Earth Charter Initiative was organized in the belief that if common values are identified and affirmed in and through a process of cross-cultural dialogue and consensus building, the danger of cultural imperialism can be avoided.

It took just over three years to complete the actual drafting of the document. During that time, the Earth Charter Commission issued two official drafts prior to the final text, the *Benchmark Draft* (March 1997) and *Benchmark Draft II* (April 1999). In addition, the drafting committee circulated many additional drafts on a trial basis.[6] These drafts were systematically revised in the light of new research and a steady flow of comments and recommendations. Hundreds of organizations and thousands of individuals from around the world became involved. Both experts and grassroots community leaders participated. Forty-five Earth Charter national committees were formed. Major regional conferences on the draft Earth Charter were held in Africa, Asia and Oceania, Central and South America, North America, and Europe. Representatives from the Middle East participated in the regional conference held in South Africa.

The drafting committee worked closely with the World Conservation Union (IUCN) Commission on Environmental Law. Workshops were held with conservation biologists and ecologists on the science-based principles. Specialists in the field of global ethics and environmental and sustainable development ethics were regularly consulted. There were ongoing discussions with representatives of the human rights movement, the international women's movement, and indigenous peoples. The Earth Charter was a central topic of discussion in a series of meetings on the theme of spirituality and sustainability held in Assisi, Italy, which were organized by the Center for Respect of Life and Environment. Earth Charter dialogues were conducted during ten international conferences on religion and ecology sponsored by the Forum on Religion and Ecology and the Center for the Study of World Religions at Harvard University and at the 1999 meeting of the Parliament of the World's Religions in Cape Town, South Africa. An extended Earth Charter dialogue took place on the Internet. In March 2000 at a meeting of the Earth Charter Commission held at the UNESCO headquarters in Paris, the drafting of the Earth Charter was completed. The document was formally launched at the Peace Palace in The Hague three months later.

During the first meeting of the Earth Charter drafting committee, which took place in January 1997, the issue arose as to how the document should refer to our planetary home. Three alternatives were considered: "the earth," "the Earth," and "Earth." The United Nations Stockholm Declaration on the Human Environment (1972) and United Nations World Charter for Nature (1982) refer to "the earth." It is also noteworthy that in these documents the term "nature" is used more extensively than "the earth." However, by the early 1990s scientists had focused attention on the environment as one great global ecosystem, in which all the parts are interconnected, and as a result in environmental reports general references to nature were increasingly replaced with specific references to "the earth" or "the Earth." Reflecting these developments, many environmentalists supported Maurice Strong's call for an Earth Charter, and the 1992 United Nations Conference on Environment and Development, which was held in Rio de Janeiro, Brazil, became known as the Rio Earth Summit. The Rio Declaration (1992), which was issued by UNCED, recognizes "the integral and interdependent nature of the Earth, our home," and it calls for protecting and restoring "the health and integrity of the Earth's ecosystem."[7] These developments led the Earth Charter drafting committee to narrow the choice to "the Earth" or "Earth."

An emphasis on respect for nature and use of "the Earth" or "Earth" in the writings of some environmentalists have led critics among religious conservatives to charge environmentalists with deifying the planet and promoting pantheism and Earth worship.[8] Even though these criticisms are for the most part without justification, the drafting committee had to keep controversies of this nature in mind. However, these concerns did not prevent the committee from deciding to capitalize Earth. One contribution was particularly helpful in this regard. Among those at the 1997 drafting meeting was an astrophysicist from Tufts University with a strong interest in global ethics, Eric Chaisson, who argued in favor of using the planet's name, Earth. He pointed out that this was common practice among his colleagues in the scientific community, none of whom was in the least bit interested in deifying the planet. All the planets in the solar system have names. When scientists speak about "earth," he said, they are referring to dirt.[9] Consultations with representatives of a worldwide network of indigenous peoples organized by the Earth Council revealed that many indigenous peoples would support use of the name Earth.

In the case under consideration, the issue facing the drafting committee was to adopt language consistent with the principle of respect for the planet and its ecosystems upon which human beings and all life are dependent for survival and development. Earth emerged as a name upon which the traditions of science and indigenous peoples could agree. That was a compelling argument for its use. However, in agreeing to adopt the name Earth without the definite article, the drafting committee was especially influenced by the way in which a change in language can influence perceptions and attitudes. When one speaks and writes about "the earth," it can perpetuate problematical, old habits of thought and behavior. There is a tendency to imagine the planet as merely a thing that is taken for granted and to view it as nothing more than a collection of resources that exists solely for the purpose of human use and exploitation. This outlook is a major factor contributing to industrial society's destructive relationship with the environment. When one begins to use the name Earth, however, it often evokes the image of the planet in space captured by the cameras of astronauts. It is an inspiring image of a beautiful, fragile, spherical island of life, humanity's only home in a vast universe that deserves our respect, love, and care.

During the first drafting meeting, Professor Chaisson also suggested that the Earth Charter include the assertion "Earth is alive" as a dramatic statement that would attract attention. Some liked the proposal because it was in the spirit of the Gaia Hypothesis put forth by James Lovelock and Lynn Margulis, and it focused attention on the biosphere as a self-regulating global ecosystem. It was also in accord with the worldview of many indigenous peoples, which was noted by Beatriz Schulthess of the Kolla Nation in Argentina. However, Holmes Rolston, an American environmental philosopher, objected to the assertion on the grounds that it was questionable from a scientific point of view. He recommended as an alternative an emphasis on the community of life. Tariq Banuri, an expert on sustainable development from Pakistan, supported the statement "Earth is alive" as a matter of "aesthetic rationality."[10] The *Benchmark Draft* states: "Earth is our home and home to all living beings. Earth itself is alive. . . ." However, the debate over this language continued as part of the larger discussion about how to refer to the planet. In the final text of the Earth Charter, the language is modified to read: "Earth, our home, is alive with a community of life." This phrasing endeavors to recognize a variety of perspectives.

During the Rio+5 Forum, which was organized by the Earth Council to assess global progress toward sustainable development and which was held in Rio de Janeiro in March 1997, leaders representing indigenous peoples recommended that the Earth Charter use the name "Mother Earth." The rights of indigenous peoples and their sustainable practices had been given special recognition by the Rio Earth Summit in Agenda 21 (chapter 26) and the Rio Declaration (Principle 22). The Earth Charter in Principles 12, 12b, and 8b affirms the rights of indigenous peoples and the value of their traditional knowledge. The *Benchmark Draft* included the statement that "Indigenous and Tribal Peoples have a vital role in the care and protection of Mother Earth." Some viewed the use of the name "Mother Earth" as simply a poetic reference that conveys deep respect. However, beginning with a press conference called by the Earth Charter Commission to launch the *Benchmark Draft*, this reference generated many questions and some objections from individuals and groups concerned about the religious and philosophical implications that use of the name might have.[11] It soon became clear that there was not wide support for this language. In later drafts, only the name "Earth" is employed.

Many writers in the environmental and sustainability movement continue to use "the Earth." This seems to reflect an interest in using the name Earth constrained by old habits of thought. It is a compromise formulation in the midst of a cultural transition involving a shift from "the earth" to "Earth." This shift is similar in a general way to the abandonment of "man" as a term for humanity as a whole and the search for gender-neutral formulations that reflect recognition and respect for women. The World Charter for Nature (1982) uses "man," but the Rio Declaration (1992) adopts gender-neutral language. Ecofeminist philosophers persuasively argue that the values of respect for women and gender equality and the values of respect for Earth and environmental conservation are interrelated.[12]

In the course of the consultation and drafting process, it became clear that a number of widely used terms and concepts should not be included. For example, a decision was made to avoid use of the term "civilization," because in the developing world, and especially in Africa, the concept had bad connotations. Colonial powers had used this term to disparage various non-Western cultures. Many advocates who support a more equitable economic world order and sustainable development promote the principle of sharing. Accordingly, the *Benchmark Draft*, which was released at the conclusion of the 1997 Rio+5 Forum in Rio de Janeiro, contains the following principle: "Share equitably the benefits of natural resource use and a healthy environment among the nations, between rich and poor, between males and females, between present and future generations. . . ." However, Pauline Tangiora, a Maori leader from New Zealand and member of the Earth Charter Commission, raised objections on behalf of indigenous peoples to any principle that calls for the sharing of resources or equitable access to resources. She and other leaders of indigenous peoples feared that such a principle could be used to pressure indigenous peoples to open their lands and resources to exploitation by international corporations. Part of the issue here was to find an ethical language that could not be easily co-opted and used to support an unethical undertaking. It was finally decided to delete language about sharing and to find other ways to express what was important regarding the value of sharing.

There were Christian, Jewish, and Islamic representatives who pressed for inclusion in the Charter of a reference to God or the Creator. However, since some religious traditions and many nonbelievers do not recognize the existence of a divine Creator, a decision was made not to use theological references. In addition, with this consideration in mind, the final version of the Charter does not employ the word "creatures" and refers to "living beings," a phrase widely used in the East and the West. However, the Commission wanted a spiritual vision in the Earth Charter that goes beyond the affirmation of ethical values. The challenge was to identify universal spiritual values and to articulate these values in a way that people with very different worldviews could endorse. One example of the way the drafting committee tried to address this challenge is the following.

The *Benchmark Draft* states that "We are humbled by the beauty of Earth and share a reverence for life and the sources of our being." When this language was not included in *Benchmark Draft II*, Leonardo Boff, a leading Latin American theologian who joined the Commission in 1999, urged the drafting committee to restore a reference to "the indispensable reverence we owe to the Ineffable Mystery, the original Source of all that is."[13] The dialogue with Boff led the drafting committee to include in the final draft of the Preamble a reference to "reverence for the mystery of being" as an important spiritual value that can strengthen commitment to a sustainable way of life.

The committee was aware that some concepts in the Earth Charter, such as "reverence for the mystery of being," could be understood in several ways by people with different worldviews. For example, the concept of "the mystery of being" can be given a completely naturalistic or a theological interpretation. "Reverence" is well defined as respect tinged with awe. For some, however, the attitude of reverence in its most profound expressions includes a sense of the sacred. The challenge was to find language that would be widely accepted and that would retain its connection with values consistent with the Earth Charter's purpose even when given varied interpretations by different cultures and traditions.

A number of organizations and philosophers, including Thomas Berry, urged that the Earth Charter affirm the rights of nature and animal rights. After a careful review, the Commissioners concluded that there was not a consensus in the global community on the use of rights language in relation to animals and ecosystems, and they were concerned that the Charter would be mired in an unproductive debate if it adopted such language. However, the Commission strongly agreed that the Charter should affirm the ethical principle that underlies the concept of the rights of nature—the idea that all species and the greater community of life deserve respect and moral consideration.

This fundamental principle of environmental protection was endorsed by the United Nations in the World Charter for Nature in 1982. The first principle of the World Charter for Nature states: "Nature shall be respected and its essential processes shall not be impaired." Its Preamble affirms that "every form of life is unique, warranting respect regardless of its worth to man, and, to accord other organisms such recognition, man must be guided by a moral code of action." These values, however, had not been reaffirmed by the Rio Earth Summit in 1992, and their absence in the Rio Declaration is one major reason why that document falls short of what environmentalists had envisioned for an Earth Charter. The Earth Charter movement has had as a primary objective to ensure that the international community recognizes respect for Earth and all life forms—nonhuman as well as human—as the foundational principle of environmental ethics and sustainable development. Five months after a final version of the Earth Charter was released by the Commission, the United Nations in the Millennium Declaration reaffirmed its commitment to the principle of "respect for nature" as one of six "fundamental values . . . essential to international relations in the twenty-first century." [14]

Following the First Principle of the Earth Charter, "Respect Earth and life in all its diversity," there is a supporting Principle 1a that endeavors to set forth the ideas on which the principle of respect for Earth and all life forms are founded. In this connection, there was a two-year debate over whether to use the term "intrinsic value." Many Western environmental philosophers endeavor to justify respect for nature by arguing that nonhuman species have intrinsic value beyond whatever instrumental or utilitarian value they may have from a human perspective.[15] In Kantian philosophical language, the point is that nonhuman species should not be regarded as merely a means to human ends, but should also be respected as ends-in-themselves. The intrinsic value of biodiversity is explicitly affirmed in the Preamble of the UN Convention on Biodiversity (1992). Early drafts of the Earth Charter directly linked respect for Earth and all life with the concept of intrinsic value.[16]

However, in some philosophical traditions the concept of intrinsic value is regarded as problematical. This is especially true in the case of the Buddhist tradition. Even though Buddhism strongly supports the principle of respect for all life, a number of Buddhist philosophers object to the assertion that all beings possess intrinsic value. They are concerned that such references can be interpreted to imply the existence of an independent fixed self, which is inconsistent with the Buddhist doctrines of emptiness (*sunyata*) and no-self. These Buddhist philosophers argue that the idea of the existence of a permanent separate self is an illusion and that the being of any life form is made up of its interrelationships with the larger world of which it is an interdependent part. The Dalai Lama has been very supportive of the Earth Charter Initiative, and among those who advised against use of the term "intrinsic value" were members of the Environment and Development Desk at his office in Dharamsala, India.[17]

As the drafting committee explored these issues, it came to realize that the idea that all life forms warrant respect and moral consideration should be linked directly with the concept of the interdependence of all beings. In other words, the principle of respect for all life is supported by the realization that all life forms are interdependent members of one great Earth community. As a general rule, all members of a human community are granted moral consideration by the community. Environmental ethics expands the sense of community and moral responsibility to embrace the whole living world. The drafting committee also recognized that the concept of the interdependence of all beings is an idea that is found in many Eastern and Western traditions. For example, it is supported in diverse ways by contemporary ecology, cosmology, and process philosophy as well as by Buddhist and Confucian philosophy.

The drafting committee further decided not to use the term "intrinsic value," given the controversy surrounding it. However, the committee was concerned to make clear that respect for nature and nonhuman species involves more than recognition that people are dependent on Earth's ecosystems and natural resources. It involves awareness that all life forms are to be valued and given moral standing even if they are not thought to have significant value for people. With all these considerations in mind, Principle 1a was revised to read: "Recognize that all beings are interdependent and every form of life has value regardless of its worth to human beings." Some environmental philosophers were disappointed that the term "intrinsic value" was not incorporated in the Earth Charter, but the new wording can be easily understood by lay people and has been widely accepted.

The *Benchmark Draft* included a Principle 15 that states: "Treat all creatures with compassion and protect them from cruelty and wanton destruction." The reference to compassion in the principle was strongly supported by the Humane Society of the United States and animal rights advocates and by Buddhists, Hindus, and Jains whose spiritual traditions put special emphasis on compassion for all living beings. However, the indigenous peoples from the circumpolar north vigorously opposed the use of the word "compassion" in this principle. This precipitated a debate that took over two years to resolve.

The chief spokespersons for the indigenous peoples who objected to the use of the word "compassion" were Finn Lynge, a representative of the Inuit Circumpolar Conference, and Henriette Rasmussen, a member of the Earth Charter Commission, who was also a member of the Greenland Home Rule Parliament and chief technical advisor at the International Labor Organization for promotion of the rights of indigenous peoples. The Inuit, who live in an environment that does not permit agriculture and who are dependent on hunting for survival, argued that it is not possible to hunt with compassion. During one meeting an Inuit leader asked: "Mr. Rockefeller, have you ever killed a whale? Do you realize what is involved?" In a letter to the drafting committee, Finn Lynge wrote:

> The word "compassion" is unacceptable among the hunting cultures be it in the arctic (Inuit/Inuppiat/Yupik, Saami, Chuckchi, Evenk, Yakut, and many more), in the sub arctic (typically e.g. the woodland Indians of Canada and Alaska), or, for example, in south-

> ern Africa. . . . If the Earth Charter is to proclaim compassion as a fundamental requirement in any morally correct dealing with other living beings, the document will be dismissed wherever the hunting cultures dominate public opinion, and the Earth Charter will fail its objective as a universal code of attitudes and conduct.[18]

There was general agreement that a person can and should hunt with respect for animals, and the Inuit Circumpolar Conference recommended to the drafting committee that the word "compassion" be replaced with "respect."[19] Not all indigenous peoples agreed with the Inuit position. Some representatives of North and South American Indians contended that it is possible to hunt with compassion. There was much good will on all sides, but the different views on the issue were passionately held.

A breakthrough in the debate came when a proposal was made to move the word "compassion" from Principle 15 to Principle 2, which is a very general principle on "care for the community of life." The Inuit indicated that they could accept the use of the word "compassion" in this context. The Buddhists, Hindus, Jains, and others who supported use of "compassion" were pleased to see the word moved to a place early in the document and attached to a principle that refers to the whole living world. It was also agreed to replace the word "compassion" with "respect" in Principle 15. In an effort to strengthen the moral force of the principle, all agreed to the addition of the noun "consideration." In the final version of the Earth Charter, Principle 15 states: "Treat all living beings with respect and consideration." The Inuit Circumpolar Conference and the Russian Association of Indigenous Peoples of the North were among the first organizations to endorse and translate the Earth Charter.

Principle 2 was expanded and states: "Care for the community of life with understanding, compassion, and love." Principles 1 and 2 are very general principles that set forth the ethic of respect and care that lies at the heart of the Earth Charter.[20] The ethical life begins with an attitude of respect, but it only takes form when respect develops into a deep sense of caring leading to action. The choice of the verb "to care for" in this context is significant. It has a broader and deeper meaning than verbs like "protect" and "conserve." "Caring" involves a person's whole being—feeling, thought, and will. The practice of caring is concerned with preventing harm and helping others. It includes tending, nurturing, and healing. The meaning of "care for the community of life" is clarified by the addition of the words "with understanding, compassion, and love." The term "understanding" in this principle means awareness, knowledge, intelligence. Human beings cannot "care for" the community of life without knowledge. However, knowledge by itself is not sufficient. Our best thought and action are inspired and guided by the integration of the head and the heart. Principle 2 joins the scientific emphasis on the role of intelligence and knowledge with the emphasis in the world's great religious traditions on the critical importance of compassion and love. The Brazilian Earth Charter national committee made a special plea in support of inclusion of a reference to "love."

During the 1980s and 1990s, there was a growing recognition at the UN and among organizations concerned with sustainable development that the environmental, economic, and social challenges facing humanity are interrelated. Holistic thinking and inclusive problem solving are essential. The Earth Charter reflects this outlook. Therefore, even though it puts special emphasis on environmental concerns, the Earth Charter includes principles on poverty eradication, human rights, gender equality, equitable economic development, democratic governance, and peace. That the Earth Charter presents an integrated ethical vision is one of its great strengths. The drafting of the social and economic principles involved lengthy discussions. Good examples are the debates surrounding the principles on gender equality and access to reproductive health care.

During the 1997 Rio+5 Forum, Bella Abzug, the founder and president of the Women's Environment and Development Organization (WEDO) and a former member of the U.S. Congress, emerged as a strong advocate in support of the Earth Charter project. She urged the drafting committee to include a principle on gender equality that states: "Affirm that gender equality is a prerequisite to sustainable development." This principle was incorporated in the

Benchmark Draft. In support of this principle, WEDO and the larger international women's movement argued that achieving gender equality was both a fundamental human rights issue and a key to achieving sustainability. They recognized that patterns of population growth in the developing world are contributing to serious environmental and social problems. However, they opposed calls for "population control" because this approach fails to focus attention on the underlying problem and can lead to oppressive social policies. The key to sustainable patterns of human reproduction, they argued, is gender equality and especially access to health care, education, and economic opportunity for women and girls. In addition, this position was endorsed by the UN summits on population (Cairo 1994) and on women (Beijing 1995), and the drafting committee was concerned to build on the international consensus achieved at important UN conferences such as these.

However, the call for gender equality met resistance from some representatives from Africa, the Middle East, and Latin America. They recommended replacing the reference to gender equality with a call for equity in the treatment of women. Equitable treatment means fair treatment. The difficulty is that what is considered equitable and fair in some traditional societies falls far short of gender equality. If the Earth Charter were to remain consistent with the ideal of universal human rights and with the Cairo and Beijing UN summits, it had to preserve Bella Abzug's original language. On the recommendation of Frene Ginwala, Speaker of the National Assembly of the Parliament of South Africa, who strongly supported the call for gender equality, a reference to equity was added to the principle. The final version of Principle 11 in the Earth Charter states: "Affirm gender equality and equity as prerequisites to sustainable development and ensure universal access to education, health care, and economic opportunity."

Given the urgent need to promote sustainable patterns of reproduction, the drafting committee was persuaded that the Earth Charter should make clear that access to health care must include access to reproductive health care. Borrowing language from the Beijing Platform for Action issued by the UN Fourth World Conference on Women (1995), the *Benchmark Draft* included a call to "secure the right to sexual and reproductive health, with special concern for women and girls." However, it soon became clear that some Christian and Islamic groups remained critical of the discussion of reproductive health in the Cairo Programme of Action and Beijing Platform, and they regarded any references to reproductive rights as an endorsement of abortion and, therefore, unacceptable. A few conservative Christian groups had come to view the adjective "reproductive" as a code word for abortion regardless of how it is used.

Extensive consultations were conducted with theologians, philosophers, and ethicists and with leaders of the international women's movement on how to handle this controversy.[21] For example, a theologian at The Vatican was consulted and offered an opinion.[22] The Commission and drafting committee agreed that the Earth Charter should not interject itself into the debate over abortion, and for this reason it was decided not to use the concept of reproductive rights in the Charter. However, a principle recognizing the need for reproductive health and healthcare was considered essential, but it was decided to make it a supporting principle rather than a main principle. In the final draft, Principle 7e states: "Ensure universal access to health care that fosters reproductive health and responsible reproduction."

The Beijing Platform defines reproductive health as "a state of complete physical, mental, and social well-being . . . in all matters relating to the reproductive system . . . ." It explains that people who enjoy reproductive health "are able to have a satisfying and safe sex life and . . . they have the capability to reproduce and the freedom to decide if, when, and how to do so."[23] The Earth Charter defines responsible reproduction in Principle 7 as patterns of reproduction "that safeguard Earth's regenerative capacities, human rights, and community well-being." Principles 1, 7, and 11 indicate that the goal of responsible reproduction should be achieved through the empowerment of women and universal access to health care, and in a fashion consistent with respect for "life in all its diversity" and respect for humanity's fundamental rights and freedoms. The Earth Charter principles make it clear that coercive methods of regulating population growth are unacceptable. Operating within the general ethical framework provided by the Earth Charter, different communities may adopt diverse approaches to the provision of reproductive health care. The Earth Charter does not attempt to address the many questions that may arise in this regard, including the question as to whether abortion may be a morally responsible choice under certain circumstances and should be a legal option.

The way the Earth Charter addresses the need for reproductive health care and responsible reproduction has been widely accepted. For example, Pax Christi International and Pax Romana, which are influential Roman Catholic organizations, eighty congregations of Roman Catholic nuns from a variety of religious orders, and the Women's Environment and Development Organization have all endorsed the Earth Charter. There are conservative religious critics who remain uncomfortable with the reference to "reproductive health" (principle 7e). However, the Earth Charter does not take a position on abortion. The Earth Charter's principles do call attention to critical ethical issues relevant to the abortion debate, and they help to frame the debate.

Early in the drafting process, Kamla Chowdhry, who was a member of the Earth Charter Commission from India and who was deeply influenced by Gandhi's spiritual philosophy and approach to human development, focused the attention of the drafting process on the importance of nonviolence as an ethical principle fundamental to a sustainable future. She opened a discussion on the subject of nonviolence during a review of an early draft with a principle on practicing peace. Kamla Chowdhry pointed out that "nonviolence is the practice and peace is the goal."[24] A consensus soon developed that the Earth Charter should emphasize nonviolence as well as peace. Consequently, the fourth and final section of Earth Charter principles was given the title "Democracy, Nonviolence, and Peace."

The concluding main Principle 16 in the Earth Charter is a call to build "a culture of tolerance, nonviolence, and peace." The principle on peace was placed last in order to make clear that enduring peace requires implementation of all the other principles. Principle 16f defines peace as "the wholeness created by right relationships with oneself, other persons, other cultures, other life, Earth, and the larger whole of which all are a part."

This essay has described a few of the many issues that came before the Earth Charter drafting committee as it conducted a worldwide, cross-cultural dialogue on shared values. One especially heartening aspect of this process was the commitment people from all regions of the world made to finding common ground. In general, when differences surfaced, those engaged in the discussion did not abandon the process, but continued to work together in the effort to articulate an ethical vision that all could embrace. The intergovernmental effort to draft an Earth Charter at Rio in 1992 failed. However, the civil society Earth Charter initiative succeeded because it was part of a growing, worldwide movement of people who recognize the urgent need for social change, global ethics, and international cooperation and who believe in the possibility of building a global community in the midst of great cultural diversity. The Earth Charter gives expression to the consensus on shared values that inspires and guides this global peoples' movement, which has become a major force alongside business and government in shaping the future.

NOTES

1. World Commission on Environment and Development, *Our Common Future* (New York: Oxford, 1987), 332.

2. For further information, see Steven C. Rockefeller, "Global Ethics, International Law and the Earth Charter," *Earth Ethics* 7 (spring/summer 1996): 1, 3–7.

3. See for example Steven C. Rockefeller, *Principles of Environmental Conservation and Sustainable Development: Summary and Survey*, A Study in the Field of International Law prepared for the Earth Charter Project, April 1996.

4. For further information, see Steven C. Rockefeller, "The Earth Charter Process," *Earth Ethics* 8 (winter/spring 1997): 3–8. For further information on the membership and procedures of the Earth Charter drafting committee see *The Earth Charter Initiative Handbook* (2000), section 5, History, printed and distributed by the international Earth Charter Secretariat, University for Peace, Costa Rica. The Earth Charter Commission appointed Steven Rockefeller to chair the drafting committee. A small core group with representatives from six countries worked closely with him on the actual writing of the text. At different times, this core group included Johannah Bernstein (Canada),

Abelardo Brenes (Costa Rica), J. Ronald Engel (USA), Brendan Mackey (Australia), Paul Raskin (USA), Mirian Vilela (Brazil), and Christine von Weizsäcker (Germany). A larger group with representatives from seventeen countries met annually between 1997 and 2000 to conduct a thorough review of the drafting process and text.

5. See "Objectives and Definitions" in the *Earth Charter Drafting Committee Book* prepared for the 4–6 January 1999 meeting; "The Earth Charter: An Overview," 15 April 1999, an unpublished document prepared for the Earth Charter Web site; and "International Drafting Committee Report," 1 March 2000, prepared by Steven C. Rockefeller for the Earth Charter Commission.

6. See for example Steven C. Rockefeller, ed., *Earth Charter Drafts, August 1995–March 1997* (Rio+5 Forum), Earth Charter Project, Earth Council, April 1997, an unpublished document prepared as a resource for the drafting committee, the Earth Council, and the Earth Charter Commission. This document contains eighteen drafts and includes reports on some of the debates and discussions surrounding these early drafts.

7. Preamble and Principle 7.

8. Criticism of the Earth Charter for promoting pantheism and Earth worship has come from several organizations, including the Catholic Family and Human Rights Institute, headed by Austin Ruse. See "UN Agency Promotes Pantheism, Denigrates Judaism, Christianity and Islam" in the *Friday Fax* issued by Austin Ruse, the director of the Institute, 30 Oct. 1998. See also the exchange between Steven Rockefeller and William F. Jasper. William F. Jasper, "The New World Religion," *New American* 18:19 (23 Sept. 2002); and Steven C. Rockefeller, letter to the editor, *New American* in response to "The New World Religion," 18:22 (4 Nov. 2002): 3.

9. See introduction, in Steven C. Rockefeller, ed., *Earth Charter Drafts, August 1995–March 1997*, 2.

10. Ibid.

11. Ibid., 2, 4.

12. See for example Rosemary Radford Ruether, *Gaia and God: An Ecofeminist Theology of Earth Healing* (San Francisco: HarperSanFrancisco, 1992; rpt. 1994).

13. Letter, Leonardo Boff to Mirian Vilela, 8 July 1999, and letter, Mirian Vilela to Steven C. Rockefeller, 9 July 1999. Steven C. Rockefeller private papers, hereafter cited as SCR private papers.

14. See United Nations Millennium Declaration, I 6. The rationale for the principle of respect for nature in this declaration includes a recognition of the need for environmental protection and sustainable development and a concern for the well-being of present and future generations. However, the concerns expressed in the rationale are entirely anthropocentric, and there is

no recognition of the intrinsic value of nonhuman species. In this regard, the statement of the principle in the Millennium Declaration is not as strong as the formulation of it in the World Charter for Nature and Earth Charter.

15. See for example Roderick Frazier Nash, *The Rights of Nature: A History of Environmental Ethics* (Madison: University of Wisconsin, 1989), and J. Baird Callicott, *In Defense of the Land Ethic: Essays in Environmental Philosophy* (Albany: SUNY, 1989).

16. See the *Benchmark Draft* issued by the Earth Charter Commission following the Rio+5 Forum in 1997.

17. See letter, His Holiness the Dalai Lama to Steven C. Rockefeller, 3 July 1999, in SCR private papers.

18. Letter, Finn Lynge to Steven C. Rockefeller, 2 Dec. 1998, in SCR private papers.

19. Ibid., and letter, Aqqaluk Lynge to members of the Earth Charter Commission c/o Earth Charter Secretariat, 21 June 1999. Aqqaluk Lynge wrote this letter as president of the Inuit Circumpolar Conference (ICC), which includes Alaskan, Canadian, Greenlandic, and Russian Inuit. In 2006 the ICC was renamed the Inuit Circumpolar Council. See letter, Aqqaluk Lynge to Steven Rockefeller, 15 Nov. 2006, in SCR private papers.

20. The principle "respect and care for the community of life" was first articulated in *Caring for the Earth: A Strategy for Sustainable Living* (Gland, Switzerland: World Conservation Union, the UN Environment Programme, and the World Wide Fund for Nature, 1991).

21. See for example letter, Patricia Mische to Steven C. Rockefeller, 5 Oct. 1998; letter, Patricia Mische to Steven C. Rockefeller, 15 Dec. 1998; and letter, Patricia Mische to Maximo Kalaw and Steven C. Rockefeller, 15 Dec. 1998; all in SCR private papers. Patricia Mische is the president of Global Education Associates (GEA), which was a partner with the Earth Council in promoting the Earth Charter consultation and drafting process. Mische assisted the drafting committee in understanding the outlook and criticisms of various Christian conservative groups, but their views did not reflect her own perspective. The mission of GEA involves promotion of deep ecology and the new cosmology, environmental sustainability, human rights, economic development, intercultural understanding, and peace. Among GEA's partner organizations are 165 Roman Catholic religious orders.

22. On behalf of the Earth Charter drafting committee, Patricia Mische consulted with Monsignor John A. Radano at the Vatican. In a letter to Patricia Mische, 26 February 1999, Mons. Radano states that the phrase "reproductive health" might be interpreted as an endorsement of abortion, "because reproductive health includes fertility regulation and according to the World Health Organization description, one method of fertility regulation does in-

clude abortion." He recommended language that includes use of the term "responsible reproduction." In SCR private papers.

23. Beijing Platform for Action (1995), Annex II, IV.c.89 and 94. Both Susan Davis and Dianne Dillon-Ridgeley, who served as director and acting director, respectively, of the Women's Environment and Development Organization, participated in drafting committee meetings and were very helpful to the committee as it worked through the issues surrounding the principles concerned with gender equality, reproductive health care, and population.

24. See introduction in Steven C. Rockefeller, ed., *Earth Charter Drafts, August 1995–March 1997*, 5.

The Earth Charter

Preamble

We stand at a critical moment in Earth's history, a time when humanity must choose its future. As the world becomes increasingly interdependent and fragile, the future at once holds great peril and great promise. To move forward we must recognize that in the midst of a magnificent diversity of cultures and life forms we are one human family and one Earth community with a common destiny. We must join together to bring forth a sustainable global society founded on respect for nature, universal human rights, economic justice, and a culture of peace. Towards this end, it is imperative that we, the peoples of Earth, declare our responsibility to one another, to the greater community of life, and to future generations.

Earth, Our Home

Humanity is part of a vast evolving universe. Earth, our home, is alive with a unique community of life. The forces of nature make existence a demanding and uncertain adventure, but Earth has provided the conditions essential to life's evolution. The resilience of the community of life and the well-being of humanity depend upon preserving a healthy biosphere with all its ecological systems, a rich variety of plants and animals, fertile soils, pure waters, and clean air. The global environment with its finite resources is a common concern of all peoples. The protection of Earth's vitality, diversity, and beauty is a sacred trust.

The Global Situation

The dominant patterns of production and consumption are causing environmental devastation, the depletion of resources, and a massive extinction of species. Communities are being undermined. The benefits of development are not shared equitably and the gap between rich and poor is widening. Injustice, poverty, ignorance, and violent conflict are widespread and the cause of great suffering. An unprecedented rise in human population has overburdened ecological and social systems. The foundations of global security are threatened. These trends are perilous—but not inevitable.

The Challenges Ahead

The choice is ours: form a global partnership to care for Earth and one another or risk the destruction of ourselves and the diversity of life. Fundamental changes are needed in our values, institutions, and ways of living. We must realize that when basic needs have been met, human development is primarily about being more, not having more. We have the knowledge and technology to provide for all and to reduce our impacts on the environment. The emergence of a global civil society is creating new opportunities to build a democratic and humane world. Our environmental, economic, political, social, and spiritual challenges are interconnected, and together we can forge inclusive solutions.

Universal Responsibility

To realize these aspirations, we must decide to live with a sense of universal responsibility, identifying ourselves with the whole Earth community as well as our local communities. We are at once citizens of different nations and of one world in which the local and global are linked. Everyone shares responsibility for the present and future well-being of the human family and the larger living world. The spirit of human solidarity and kinship with all life is strengthened when we live with reverence for the mystery of being, gratitude for the gift of life, and humility regarding the human place in nature.

We urgently need a shared vision of basic values to provide an ethical foundation for the emerging world community. Therefore, together in hope we affirm the following interdependent principles for a sustainable way of life as a common standard by which the conduct of all individuals, organizations, businesses, governments, and transnational institutions is to be guided and assessed.

Principles

I. Respect and Care for the Community of Life

1. Respect Earth and life in all its diversity.
   a. Recognize that all beings are interdependent and every form of life has value regardless of its worth to human beings.
   b. Affirm faith in the inherent dignity of all human beings and in the intellectual, artistic, ethical, and spiritual potential of humanity.
2. Care for the community of life with understanding, compassion, and love.
   a. Accept that with the right to own, manage, and use natural resources comes the duty to prevent environmental harm and to protect the rights of people.
   b. Affirm that with increased freedom, knowledge, and power comes increased responsibility to promote the common good.
3. Build democratic societies that are just, participatory, sustainable, and peaceful.
   a. Ensure that communities at all levels guarantee human rights and fundamental freedoms and provide everyone an opportunity to realize his or her full potential.
   b. Promote social and economic justice, enabling all to achieve a secure and meaningful livelihood that is ecologically responsible.

4. Secure Earth's bounty and beauty for present and future generations.
    a. Recognize that the freedom of action of each generation is qualified by the needs of future generations.
    b. Transmit to future generations values, traditions, and institutions that support the long-term flourishing of Earth's human and ecological communities.

In order to fulfill these four broad commitments, it is necessary to:

II. Ecological Integrity

5. Protect and restore the integrity of Earth's ecological systems, with special concern for biological diversity and the natural processes that sustain life.
    a. Adopt at all levels sustainable development plans and regulations that make environmental conservation and rehabilitation integral to all development initiatives.
    b. Establish and safeguard viable nature and biosphere reserves, including wild lands and marine areas, to protect Earth's life support systems, maintain biodiversity, and preserve our natural heritage.
    c. Promote the recovery of endangered species and ecosystems.
    d. Control and eradicate non-native or genetically modified organisms harmful to native species and the environment, and prevent introduction of such harmful organisms.
    e. Manage the use of renewable resources such as water, soil, forest products, and marine life in ways that do not exceed rates of regeneration and that protect the health of ecosystems.
    f. Manage the extraction and use of non-renewable resources such as minerals and fossil fuels in ways that minimize depletion and cause no serious environmental damage.
6. Prevent harm as the best method of environmental protection and, when knowledge is limited, apply a precautionary approach.

a. Take action to avoid the possibility of serious or irreversible environmental harm even when scientific knowledge is incomplete or inconclusive.
b. Place the burden of proof on those who argue that a proposed activity will not cause significant harm, and make the responsible parties liable for environmental harm.
c. Ensure that decision making addresses the cumulative, long-term, indirect, long distance, and global consequences of human activities.
d. Prevent pollution of any part of the environment and allow no build-up of radioactive, toxic, or other hazardous substances.
e. Avoid military activities damaging to the environment.

7. Adopt patterns of production, consumption, and reproduction that safeguard Earth's regenerative capacities, human rights, and community well-being.
   a. Reduce, reuse, and recycle the materials used in production and consumption systems, and ensure that residual waste can be assimilated by ecological systems.
   b. Act with restraint and efficiency when using energy, and rely increasingly on renewable energy sources such as solar and wind.
   c. Promote the development, adoption, and equitable transfer of environmentally sound technologies.
   d. Internalize the full environmental and social costs of goods and services in the selling price, and enable consumers to identify products that meet the highest social and environmental standards.
   e. Ensure universal access to health care that fosters reproductive health and responsible reproduction.
   f. Adopt lifestyles that emphasize the quality of life and material sufficiency in a finite world.
8. Advance the study of ecological sustainability and promote the open exchange and wide application of the knowledge acquired.

a. Support international scientific and technical cooperation on sustainability, with special attention to the needs of developing nations.
b. Recognize and preserve the traditional knowledge and spiritual wisdom in all cultures that contribute to environmental protection and human well-being.
c. Ensure that information of vital importance to human health and environmental protection, including genetic information, remains available in the public domain.

III. Social and Economic Justice

9. Eradicate poverty as an ethical, social, and environmental imperative.
   a. Guarantee the right to potable water, clean air, food security, uncontaminated soil, shelter, and safe sanitation, allocating the national and international resources required.
   b. Empower every human being with the education and resources to secure a sustainable livelihood, and provide social security and safety nets for those who are unable to support themselves.
   c. Recognize the ignored, protect the vulnerable, serve those who suffer, and enable them to develop their capacities and to pursue their aspirations.
10. Ensure that economic activities and institutions at all levels promote human development in an equitable and sustainable manner.
   a. Promote the equitable distribution of wealth within nations and among nations.
   b. Enhance the intellectual, financial, technical, and social resources of developing nations, and relieve them of onerous international debt.
   c. Ensure that all trade supports sustainable resource use, environmental protection, and progressive labor standards.
   d. Require multinational corporations and international financial organizations to act transparently in the public

good, and hold them accountable for the consequences of their activities.

11. Affirm gender equality and equity as prerequisites to sustainable development and ensure universal access to education, health care, and economic opportunity.
    a. Secure the human rights of women and girls and end all violence against them.
    b. Promote the active participation of women in all aspects of economic, political, civil, social, and cultural life as full and equal partners, decision makers, leaders, and beneficiaries.
    c. Strengthen families and ensure the safety and loving nurture of all family members.
12. Uphold the right of all, without discrimination, to a natural and social environment supportive of human dignity, bodily health, and spiritual well-being, with special attention to the rights of indigenous peoples and minorities.
    a. Eliminate discrimination in all its forms, such as that based on race, color, sex, sexual orientation, religion, language, and national, ethnic or social origin.
    b. Affirm the right of indigenous peoples to their spirituality, knowledge, lands and resources and to their related practice of sustainable livelihoods.
    c. Honor and support the young people of our communities, enabling them to fulfill their essential role in creating sustainable societies.
    d. Protect and restore outstanding places of cultural and spiritual significance.

IV. Democracy, Nonviolence, and Peace

13. Strengthen democratic institutions at all levels, and provide transparency and accountability in governance, inclusive participation in decision making, and access to justice.
    a. Uphold the right of everyone to receive clear and timely information on environmental matters and all

development plans and activities which are likely to affect them or in which they have an interest.

b. Support local, regional and global civil society, and promote the meaningful participation of all interested individuals and organizations in decision making.

c. Protect the rights to freedom of opinion, expression, peaceful assembly, association, and dissent.

d. Institute effective and efficient access to administrative and independent judicial procedures, including remedies and redress for environmental harm and the threat of such harm.

e. Eliminate corruption in all public and private institutions.

f. Strengthen local communities, enabling them to care for their environments, and assign environmental responsibilities to the levels of government where they can be carried out most effectively.

14. Integrate into formal education and life-long learning the knowledge, values, and skills needed for a sustainable way of life.

a. Provide all, especially children and youth, with educational opportunities that empower them to contribute actively to sustainable development.

b. Promote the contribution of the arts and humanities as well as the sciences in sustainability education.

c. Enhance the role of the mass media in raising awareness of ecological and social challenges.

d. Recognize the importance of moral and spiritual education for sustainable living.

15. Treat all living beings with respect and consideration.

a. Prevent cruelty to animals kept in human societies and protect them from suffering.

b. Protect wild animals from methods of hunting, trapping, and fishing that cause extreme, prolonged, or avoidable suffering.

c. Avoid or eliminate to the full extent possible the taking or destruction of non-targeted species.

16. Promote a culture of tolerance, nonviolence, and peace.
    a. Encourage and support mutual understanding, solidarity, and cooperation among all peoples and within and among nations.
    b. Implement comprehensive strategies to prevent violent conflict and use collaborative problem solving to manage and resolve environmental conflicts and other disputes.
    c. Demilitarize national security systems to the level of a non-provocative defense posture, and convert military resources to peaceful purposes, including ecological restoration.
    d. Eliminate nuclear, biological, and toxic weapons and other weapons of mass destruction.
    e. Ensure that the use of orbital and outer space supports environmental protection and peace.
    f. Recognize that peace is the wholeness created by right relationships with oneself, other persons, other cultures, other life, Earth, and the larger whole of which all are a part.

The Way Forward

As never before in history, common destiny beckons us to seek a new beginning. Such renewal is the promise of these Earth Charter principles. To fulfill this promise, we must commit ourselves to adopt and promote the values and objectives of the Charter.

This requires a change of mind and heart. It requires a new sense of global interdependence and universal responsibility. We must imaginatively develop and apply the vision of a sustainable way of life locally, nationally, regionally, and globally. Our cultural diversity is a precious heritage and different cultures will find their own distinctive ways to realize the vision. We must deepen and expand the global dialogue that generated the Earth Charter, for we have much to learn from the ongoing collaborative search for truth and wisdom.

Life often involves tensions between important values. This can mean difficult choices. However, we must find ways to harmonize diversity with unity, the exercise of freedom with the common good, short-term objectives with long-term goals. Every individual, family, organization, and community has a vital role to play. The arts, sciences, religions, educational institutions, media, businesses, nongovernmental organizations, and governments are all called to offer creative leadership. The partnership of government, civil society, and business is essential for effective governance.

In order to build a sustainable global community, the nations of the world must renew their commitment to the United Nations, fulfill their obligations under existing international agreements, and support the implementation of Earth Charter principles with an international legally binding instrument on environment and development.

Let ours be a time remembered for the awakening of a new reverence for life, the firm resolve to achieve sustainability, the quickening of the struggle for justice and peace, and the joyful celebration of life.

NOTE

Available online at http://www.earthcharter.org/.

Principle into Imagination

Literary Responses to the Earth Charter

Owning the Imperatives

A Poem for the Earth Charter

Alison Hawthorne Deming

1
Respect the doctrine of the sun-warm Earth where life lifts sweet and peppery into the sky reaching for something warmer until it stops and knows its home

2
Care for all the rooms of the house, especially the one where the dust and unpacked boxes are piled because what is flawed and unfinished teaches what is sacred

3
Build a council table for the factions in the mind that disagree with dreams of human kindness

4
Secure the doors of wildness (the bedroom where descendents sleep) against attack

5
Protect and restore the future as a neighborhood where children want to live

6
Prevent lies and crimes from visiting as virtues in disguise

7
Adopt the ravine where tule elks graze the burn where Bishop's
pines release their fire-hearty seeds the relict forest where wren-
tit monkeyflower ceanothus rebound the vista on the mountain
trail where bobcat leaves his daily scat the filth where flukes and
flatworms feed the canyon winds older than life because love even
when held only in mind creates spiritual effects in the world our
wounded mother unbroken continuous whole

8
Advance the science of the ancients which is gratitude and let no
one own the common wealth of attention paid to the real

9
Eradicate the desperation of the poor by swapping anger, alleyways
and ashcans for books, bicycles and bags of wheat

10
Ensure that each person in the family has the choice (the old one
the crazy the poor the child) whether to eat alone in her room or
go hungry or join the table set for company

11
Affirm the body as a deer path along which evolution runs lost in
the pleasure of leap stretch and scent, each creature a sheltering
habitat for that force, each habitat an equal source of wisdom

12
Uphold the oldest family stories (pasture trail savannah cave) as
the clay from which you and your house are made

13
Strengthen the patience of children so they learn to listen for the
quiet voices

14
Integrate windows (for beauty) and doorways (for possibilities) into
household renovations

15
Treat animals as if they understood complexity better than human beings do, treat human beings as if they understood kindness better than complexity

16
Promote collective good whenever it speaks with a clear voice, invite it indoors no matter if it wears the clothes of anger, shame, poverty, grief, for given shelter it may leave those garments with its weapons at the door and dress to take its place at the family table

Learning to See the Stars

The Earth Charter as a Compass for the New Century

Mary Evelyn Tucker

Voyages of recovery

Some years ago in Hawai'i I attended an International World History Conference that was organized around the theme of oceans in world history. At the opening dinner of the conference Nainoa Thompson, a young Hawaiian sail master with the Polynesian Voyaging Society, told the story of the Hokulea voyages that re-created the earlier Pacific journeys from Hawai'i south to Tahiti. These voyages took place in the centuries of great oceanic migrations in the Pacific from approximately 700 AD to 1400 AD. *Hokulea* is the name given to the canoe built for these voyages and is translated as "Star of Gladness" for a star that passes over Hawai'i.

Here we were two hundred academics sitting in a windowless banquet room with the usual generic hotel décor—high ceilings, heavy curtains, glitzy chandeliers, and predictable carpets. The speaker had been appropriately introduced and bedecked with a lei, the slides were in place, and his soft voice proceeded to narrate. Almost like an ancient Hawaiian chant his story began to unfold from this unassuming slight man before us. He began with disclaimers and modest apologies and then proceeded to electrify the audience with his verbal and visual images of the journey.

"We wanted to re-create the original sea voyages of our ancestors from Hawai'i back to the South Pacific islands," he began. "They had been stopped for hundreds of years due to a mysterious taboo. We wanted to reconstruct the original outrigger canoes and to bring along only traditional foods.

"First we needed a navigator. We searched among our own Hawaiian people but no one emerged as knowledgeable enough to guide us across these vast ocean distances. We sent word down to the South Pacific that some of us Hawaiians wanted to relearn the traditional navigation techniques. One of the last 'ancient mariners' of the South Pacific replied. Named Mao Pilaug, he came up to Hawai'i from the Melanesian island of Satawal.

"Mao began to help us with the building of the canoe and with outfitting it. But most importantly he began to share with us his knowledge of how to sail it. Slowly we began to read the flotsam and plankton on the surface of the sea. Little by little we began to notice the patterns of birds' flight. We started to feel the movements of the waves and the direction of the currents. Eventually we learned to see the map of the stars on the low horizon and learned how to read it, providing us with direction. Gradually we discovered how to see the sun and to place its rising and its setting in relation to sea movements and sky constellations. We felt the voyage being born within us.

"We set out onto the high seas with two canoes and a crew of nine people. It was far from perfect, but we learned as we sailed—about human nature and conflict and cooperation, about Mother Nature and vulnerability and humility. We read the position of the sun and the stars, and discerned the movements of the currents and the waves. Without compass or modern technology we proceeded across the paths of our ancestors. We were both exhilarated and exhausted.

"Our challenges came quickly and sometimes unexpectedly. The most difficult was navigating on a cloudy or stormy night. With no moon or stars, it was impossible for us to continue to sail. It was especially at these difficult points that we had to call on the ancient mariner. On those dark, cloud-filled nights in the midst of this vast Pacific Ocean Mao would go and lie in the hull of the canoe. As was the custom with children in Melanesia he had spent much of his early childhood in a canoe—sometimes simply rocked in a canoe tied to the shore like a cradle, sometimes accompanying a family member on a fishing expedition. From both instincts absorbed as a child and knowledge taught by his elders, he could feel the swell of the waves and discern the movement of the currents. He would navigate our direction based on these ancient indigenous ways of knowing that had been learned and transmitted across the centuries. We were deeply moved in witnessing this."

The narrator, Nainoa Thompson, told how he had to adjust much of his scientific training and constrain his "modern" skepticism to learn these ancient navigation techniques. But he acknowledged he had still not reached into the instinctual indigenous knowledge of reading the waves from the depths of the hull.

The story of the Hokulea journey can be viewed as a metaphor for our own need to recover and discover paths over vast tracks of uncharted waters toward a sustainable future. We are like the ancient mariner in a cloudy night trying to navigate our way into a new historical moment when humans will contribute to the flourishing of the Earth community, not to its destruction.

In this process the Earth Charter as a comprehensive global ethic serves as a compass to guide humans in such a new and creative venture. The Preamble and the Principles of the Charter act like a constellation of stars illuminating the voyage. "The Way Forward" provides a sense of destiny and commitment beckoning humans to build a sustainable global community. My participation in the drafting of the charter has a long history, including over three decades of studying other cultures and religions, first by living in Japan and then by nearly a decade of graduate studies at Columbia University. My search has always been for the way in which we can create a vision of a common future that will honor both cultural and biological diversity, or, in the words of the Earth Charter, "to live with a sense of universal responsibility, identifying ourselves with the whole Earth community as well as our local communities."[1] Like the Hawaiians, I had to cross the Pacific to find my way, bringing traditional values to bear on modern concerns like ecology and equity.

Voyages of discovery

More than thirty years ago I took a voyage across the Pacific—but my direction was from the West to the East. At the same time the Hawaiians were recovering their transoceanic routes of discovery from south to north, I was discovering traditional values of Asian civilization. I was young, innocent, and largely ignorant of Asian cultures. College had not prepared me for the vast differences of worldview I would experience. No classes had opened up the doors to the rich civilizations that I encountered, first in Japan and then in other parts of Asia. But I had begun to experience the emerging planetary civilization that was arising from human exchanges across cultures on a scale never before possible. My journey toward the Earth Charter was underway.

In college I had traveled to England where I lived for a year at Oxford. I roamed England and the continent like a hungry child in search of the feast of culture, art, and history that Europe so readily provides. But even this journey into the heart of western European civilization could not have prepared me for Japan—an island country, like England, but one located on the other side of the Eurasian continent. Densely packed with people and steeped in traditional ways, Japan was still in the grips of its own postwar history. Yet it was already caught in the tensions of traditional customs and modern aspirations. This would both fascinate and confuse me as I plunged into this unknown archipelago. Indeed, I had to climb a gate to enter.

I had traveled for seemingly endless hours across the Pacific in a small plane. I arrived alone late at night at Haneda airport and took an hour-long taxi ride through the winding streets of Tokyo. The convent gate where I would be staying was locked, and there was nothing to be done but climb over. The taxi driver was dumbfounded, watching with silent amazement this tall, foreign woman scale the gate. I walked up to the door and rang the bell. To this day I am amused by the fact that the woman who answered the door and walked back to unlock the gate to retrieve my luggage never asked how I had gotten in.

My experience of Japan was thus literally as well as figuratively climbing over a high wall to enter a different culture. The Earth Charter explains that "We are at once citizens of different nations and of one world in which the local and the global are linked."[2] Having not yet bridged the gap between my own culture and other cultures, I was completely disoriented during my early days in Japan. The challenges were many and diverse as I was an unusually tall woman with auburn hair and blue eyes in a country where drivers' licenses don't indicate hair and eye color because they are uniformly the same. Even within the protective walls of the university where I was teaching I was an oddity. On the street corners people would stare at me and point as they were not used to seeing foreigners. It was like being in *Gulliver's Travels*.

I had come to teach English language and literature at a university in Okayama, a castle town between Kyoto and Hiroshima on the Inland Sea. As I stood before the class, alone on a raised platform, my height was further accentuated. The students were all women who wore identical uniforms, and their names were hard to remember. They were intrigued to learn English, but it was I who learned from them.

They taught me about the cultural habits that made this heterogeneous society work smoothly—the way people bowed and greeted one another, the politeness of phrase and expression, the gift giving and receiving with carefully considered proportionality. These deeply embedded ritual patterns of exchange fascinated me. Realizing too that a foreigner could never fully enter this web of human relations was daunting.

Nonetheless, as I tried with authenticity to lower myself gradually over the wall of cultural differences, I found myself accepted as more than a cultural oddity. I moved into a space of reciprocity, embraced by a web of human relations and values more intricate than I could fully understand. The tenderness and depths of friendships that opened up were truly astonishing. The wall disappeared, and human affectivity flowed through the channels of ritual formality and into a giving and shared presence of person to person that was intense and heartfelt. The space of our common humanity held us in a new pattern of respect, opening us up to a shared future not possible for our parents' generation locked in a time of war. Difference was overcome in the space of shared concerns.

In wandering about through the maze of human relations on the other side of the wall I became intrigued by family interactions, student-teacher exchanges, friendship bonds, as well as by more impersonal encounters in stores and public places. What was it that made this all work? What was the social glue that seemed to hold the society together? What kept the crime rate so low and a sense of respect for neighbors so widespread? What could we in the West learn from Japanese values?

Although I studied Zen Buddhism intensively and read widely in Shinto, I eventually discovered that Confucian ethics governed these ritualized exchanges. Confucianism involves a system of mutual rites and responsibilities organized around an intricate understanding of individual roles within a social network and hierarchy. The sense of traditional Confucian values guiding Japanese society was omnipresent. The values were intuited and taught by example, as well as embedded in the educational system. Their pervasive presence was like a cultural DNA passed on from generation to generation. These Confucian habits of the heart that imprinted Japanese society for more than a millennium had moved across East Asia from China through Korea to Japan. These traditions were strong even in the early 1970s in Japan.

But some of these values that held the society so tightly bound were beginning to unravel. Just as the Japanese made their way out of the Meiji era with the opening of the country by Commodore Perry, so now they were finding a path forward into new cultural values as the western world began to press in once again. The postwar industrialization and accompanying economic prosperity had provided the opportunity for the Japanese to look both inward and outward.

Inwardly Confucian conformity to tradition and to group loyalty was being challenged by the press of modernity and the appeal of western individualism. Could group pressures overcome the yearning for personal freedoms? Disaffected youths with spiked and colored hair were gathering at Harajuku in Tokyo. Artists sought different modes of expression. The security of lifetime employment in large corporations was diminishing. Women were searching for roles outside the family. Something new was emerging—a fusion of values and attitudes that drew on both tradition and modernity.

As they looked outward the Japanese were beginning to envision a new kind of *kokusaiteki shiso* or "international thinking" that would challenge some of their nationalistic loyalties. How could they weave together the sense of their own uniqueness as a nation and as a people (*Nihonjinron*) with a perceived need to join the international community? The phrase *ware ware Nihonhonjin* ("we Japanese") was frequently used to illustrate the dividing line with those in the rest of the world who were labeled *gaijin* ("foreigners"). All those who were not ethnic Japanese, no matter how long they had lived in Japan, were considered foreigners.

As an American in Japan in the early 1970s I was bewildered by this category of "foreigner" because the United States is a country based, at least in principle, on an acceptance of people with diverse ethnic backgrounds. The common myth is that anyone can become an American. As imperfect as the melting pot ideal has been in our relatively short national history, it at least aspires toward the values of providing a basis for "liberty, equality, and fraternity." Our nationalism, while often invoked for narrow and jingoistic ends, can also embrace difference. We are moving gradually from exclusion to inclusion of peoples. This is an ongoing process still with immense defects, as many minority groups will attest. And this same challenge is widespread around the world.

These vexing questions of personal liberties and public responsibilities, of inclusion and exclusion, of nationalism and internationalism are ones that both Japan and America have struggled to resolve. These experiences in Japan led me to ponder how we could begin to create the basis for a multiform planetary civilization, a new global civil society. Different cultural and ethical values need to be respected while a sense of a common and sustainable future is created. Negotiating how to protect both cultural diversity and biodiversity is a new task at hand.

What could this be based on? What kind of appeal could be made to respect cultural differences and protect the planet's resources for present and future generations? Was a clash of civilizations inevitable? As I traveled to other parts of Asia over the next thirty years I saw the immense variety of cultural diversity while witnessing the steady erosion of the environment. Cities like Bangkok and Delhi that were livable in the 1970s became increasingly polluted and congested in the 1980s and 1990s. How would the press of peoples into cities and the growing competition for resources be resolved? It was overwhelming to contemplate. And as China and India began to modernize and industrialize, what would happen to the planet and its limited resources? Over two billion people in these countries were now eager to acquire cars, refrigerators, energy, and luxury products. Was development actually sustainable? What could the world's cultures and religions contribute to an ethics of ecology and equity? Could we overcome our differences as humans to chart a course into the next stages of human history?

My journey, then, across the Pacific to Asia is one that has shaped my global outlook in countless ways. Just as the Hawaiians were recovering their own traditional values and environmental knowledge, so too the discovery of Asian values for westerners like myself was opening up the possibility for creating a new multiform global ethics. This was broadened and deepened with new college courses and translations of classical and modern texts that many of us in non-western studies have helped to create. The dialogue of civilizations was indeed growing. The Earth Charter, then, was already emerging in these cross-cultural exchanges of recovery and discovery that distinguished the postwar period.

Navigating our way forward

There has been no period in human history like these past sixty years when cultures have been able to interact on such a global scale. At the same time the threats to the planet's ecosystems and life forms have never been more pressing as industrialization has swept around the planet. In the twentieth century we exploded from two billion people to over six billion people, causing consumption levels to also spiral upward. There is an urgency about our present moment as we are realizing that our global environmental crisis is of a magnitude never before imagined. Its manifestations in climate change and species extinction are cause for concern for the future of all life. Is biocide or ecocide now possible? If so, how can this be avoided?

There is a profound sense emerging around the globe that we are at a critical moment of transition and transformation. The Earth Charter recognizes this and suggests that our present economic mode of unlimited growth and unrestrained development is no longer viable. The increasing social gap between the rich and the poor is seen as no longer acceptable. The mindless ravaging of resources and the conscious abuse of human rights are recognized as no longer tolerable. How then to realign our priorities and values within the human community for the enhancement of the larger Earth community remains the fundamental challenge of the Earth Charter.

The Earth Charter represents an historic effort to articulate the aspirations of humanity yearning for a peaceful, secure, and sustainable future. It is both a process for articulating an ethical path that respects difference and a document for upholding common principles for mutual cooperation. It is a context for constructing a multiform planetary civilization. This requires a new integration of the values of the world's cultures and religions along with the contributions of modern science and technology. This inclusive ethical vision of the Earth Charter encourages us to move into the new millennium with an energized sense of our particular human role in the evolution of the universe and Earth.

The voyage of drafting

How to bring together a culturally and religiously diverse set of values to bear on our global environmental crisis was one of the principal tasks of the International Drafting Committee for the Earth Charter. My participation on that Committee was an extraordinary experience of the creative efforts of citizens from many countries and cultures to help shape a dialogue of civilizations toward a sustainable future. The Committee's multiyear negotiations involved conversations with thousands of people from around the planet. The negotiations recognized that such dialogue depended on affirming the potential force of global civil society and the interdependence of our planetary problems. As the Preamble states: "The emergence of a global civil society is creating new opportunities to build a democratic and humane world. Our environmental, economic, political, social, and spiritual challenges are interconnected and together we can forge inclusive solutions."[3]

To accomplish this, the Earth Charter observes that we need to "Recognize and preserve the traditional knowledge and spiritual wisdom in all cultures that contribute to environmental protection and human well-being."[4] To identify this kind of knowledge was one of the primary aims of the World Religions and Ecology conference series held from 1996 to 1998 at the Center for the Study of World Religions at Harvard Divinity School. During this period a draft of the Earth Charter was circulated for discussion among the hundreds of participants. One of the most recurring discussions in the different conferences was reflection on the various modes of human-Earth interdependence evident in the traditions. In this vein, values from each of the religions were considered regarding attitudes and practices toward nature and toward other species both historically and at present.

The ongoing debate concerning the inherent value of nature, for example, was given distinctive expression when the Buddhists suggested the phrase "every form of life has value regardless of its worth to human beings."[5] Likewise, the Dalai Lama contributed the concept of "universal responsibility" in contrast to an individual rights approach to planetary life.[6] Moreover, Jain and Hindu representatives promoted the value of nonviolence (*ahimsa*). Indigenous peoples called for recognition of their spiritual and human rights, as well as respect for their sustainable livelihood practices.

This carefully considered inclusion of cultural and religious perspectives was brought together with the best of current scientific and ecological knowledge. This was especially highlighted in the writing of the Preamble. We had gathered on a beautiful autumn morning at the Pocantico Conference Center in Tarrytown, New York, for one of the first meetings of the Drafting Committee. Eric Chaisson, an astrophysicist from Tufts and Harvard Universities, was part of a three-person subgroup working on the Preamble, which included the Confucian scholar from Harvard, Tu Weiming, and myself. Eric suggested the sentences: "Humanity is part of a vast evolving universe. Earth, our home, is alive with a unique community of life."[7] The first sentence was intended to include an evolutionary perspective in the Earth Charter while the second makes a reference to the Gaia hypothesis of Earth as an alive, self-regulating entity.

What was especially striking was that Beatriz Schulthess, an indigenous Mayan representative on the Drafting Committee, was deeply moved that the phrase "Earth, our home, is alive" was included in the Preamble. When the draft was brought to Rio in March 1997 the fact that this phrase remained in the text was for her, and for other native peoples, of singular importance. Indeed, when Mikhail Gorbachev held up the text for the five hundred assembled delegates to adopt, Beatriz wept for joy. For the first time in an international document of this kind the perspective of indigenous peoples was included. It was an historic moment for them and for all of us.

This story represents something of the remarkable process involved in the creation of the Earth Charter. The continued efforts to be culturally inclusive and religiously sensitive were noteworthy. How to craft a document that would be effective in identifying universal principles for a sustainable future and that would have an appeal across cultures was a challenge of significant proportions. The Earth Charter calls for such a spirit of unity amidst diversity: "To move forward we must recognize that in the midst of a magnificent diversity of cultures and life forms we are one human family and one Earth community with a common destiny."[8]

Conclusion

What is significant about the Earth Charter is that it draws on both the comprehensive context of evolution and ecology and the empowering context of an inclusive environmental and social ethics. The Preamble contains the phrase: "The forces of nature make existence a demanding and uncertain adventure, but Earth has provided the conditions essential to life's evolution."[9] The Earth Charter thus affirms that the physical, chemical, and biological conditions for evolution are in delicate interaction over time to bring forth and sustain life. Our response to this dynamic process is responsibility for its continuity. We are called to become a life-enhancing species.

Responsibility requires an integrated and empowering framework where humans can see causal relationships of problems along with interconnected solutions. This is what the Earth Charter aims to do as it delineates a viable blueprint for a sustainable future. It highlights the interlinked issues of environment, justice, and peace as at the heart of our global challenges. Against the comprehensive background of evolution in the Preamble, the main body of the Earth Charter outlines an integrated set of ethics and practices to address these three interrelated issues. It aims to address the sometimes competing areas of environment and development that together constituted the principal theme of the Earth Summit in Rio.

The Earth Charter begins and ends on a challenging note, stating: "The foundations of global security are threatened"; however, it observes: "These trends are perilous—but not inevitable."[10] The Earth Charter suggests: "The choice is ours: form a global partnership to care for Earth and one another or risk the destruction of ourselves and the diversity of life."[11] It concludes with a similarly challenging but cautiously optimistic tone: "As never before in history, common destiny beckons us to seek a new beginning."[12] It notes that "This requires a change of mind and heart"—of vision and values.[13]

The Earth Charter, then, exemplifies an important contemporary trend toward identifying an integrative global ethics. Within the comprehensive framework of evolutionary history it highlights the significance of our moment in human history. It provides an empowering context of values and practices that will steer the human community forward toward the enhancement, not the diminishment of life. Further reflection on the Earth Charter in political gatherings, religious groups, academic settings, business offices, and environmental organizations is already well underway. In these contexts the Earth Charter acts as a framework for engagement in mutually enhancing human-Earth relations. To imagine, inspire, and activate these relations is to bring into being the contours of a multiform planetary civilization.

After he finished narrating his story about the recovery of ancient seafaring knowledge, Nainoa Thompson highlighted its contemporary import. He told us how the voyagers were eager to share their experiences with the children in the Hawaiian schools. In later voyages the classrooms were linked up to the Hokulea canoes by solar technology. The Hawaiian children could relay their questions on geography and astronomy to the crew who then answered them. Through modern technology the children were connected to a contemporary voyage that held the past in its wake and the future in its wave-shattering foam.

Just as the Hawaiian children were encouraged and inspired by sharing in this ancestral journey so, too, were several thousand natives who gathered to welcome the Hokulea canoes when they sailed into the bay in Tahiti. The Tahitians greeted the voyagers with their ancient melodic chants of welcome and the Hawaiians replied with their own traditional chants acknowledging their hosts. Across the gap of many centuries these ancient journeys were renewed and the peoples of the Pacific revitalized, learning to read the stars and the ocean in a new way.

Like the Hawaiians, we can call on both indigenous navigational knowledge and modern solar technology in our journey. For we are in the process of creating a multiform, planetary civilization drawing on wisdom that is traditional and modern, ancient and contemporary. As we are identifying the various cultural and religious values in the human community that will create the foundations for a sustainable Earth community, the Earth Charter can act as a compass for navigating our way into this promising future.

NOTES

1. Earth Charter, Preamble, paragraph five.
2. Earth Charter, Preamble, paragraph five.
3. Earth Charter, Preamble, paragraph four.

4. Earth Charter, Subprinciple 8b.
5. Earth Charter, Subprinciple 1a.
6. Earth Charter, Preamble, paragraph five.
7. Earth Charter, Preamble, paragraph two.
8. Earth Charter, Preamble, paragraph one.
9. Earth Charter, Preamble, paragraph two.
10. Earth Charter, Preamble, paragraph three.
11. Earth Charter, Preamble, paragraph four.
12. Earth Charter, The Way Forward, paragraph one.
13. Earth Charter, The Way Forward, paragraph two.

Remembering the Ancient Path

The Original Instructions and the Earth Charter

Chief Jake Swamp

The Earth Charter is the most important document in our time, as humans living on Planet Earth. It is important for several reasons. It is a way to open the human eyes so that every living thing will have value, spiritual value. It is a way to open the human heart so that nature will find a home. The human will finally learn to give thanks every day to all of creation. From the very souls of men and women and all of the children we can learn to give thanks.

We can offer special thanks every day to our ancient Mother, Earth. We can thank the smallest insect to the largest trees in the world. We can thank the water, grasses, fruits and berries, medicinal herbs, animals, and birds. We can send our thanks to the four winds, the rain, sun, moon, and stars, and to our great Creator for giving us this beautiful planet to live on.

Native American communities are small in size but large in the reach of their extended families. Those connections transcend political, territorial, and temporal barriers. We are connected not only to our immediate relatives but also to all those generations before us. We also have a special responsibility to the generations to come. In the way of the Haudenosaunee—the people of the long house—we believe that we are also connected to all of the Native Americans through clan and common experiences. While it is difficult to generalize Native American beliefs and experiences because each community has its unique identity, way of being, and history, we do have shared memories that connect us.

For the Haudenosaunee, both past and present, these shared memories link us to our ancestors. In one sense we can still see their footprints on this earth. They laid out a path for us to follow. It is not an actual trail, but is the shared memory of why we are walking on the same path of life that they did. We call this path the Original Instructions. The instructions have become our shared memories about how humans are to conduct themselves on this land we call North America. These instructions provide a frame of reference for looking at our relationship to the sacred universe—our first extended family. The celestial beings are our relatives. They are alive with spirit, just as we are. We are connected to a great web of life. In that life there is no racism, no prejudice, no discrimination. There is only thc common human duty to do good in this world.

The Original Instructions also discuss our relationship to Earth, our original mother, who continues to support us as we walk about. Our long-term health and well-being are dependent upon the health and well-being of Earth. Our instructions also explain our relationships to the plants, animals, fish, birds, and other creatures with whom we share this great place of life. Our shared memories of the past explain very clearly the relationship of people to one another. This web of life includes all living creatures, all peoples of the world.

The path of the Original Instructions is echoed in the Earth Charter. In many ways, relationships between people, communities, cultures, and nations are predicated upon three simple values.

First, we are to love each other as if we are members of one large, extended family. However, our concept of family is not to have a father in charge of the wife and children. Instead, the whole family is interconnected, dependent upon each member to fulfill its responsibilities to the well-being of the entire family. As the Earth Charter says, we must "Strengthen families and ensure the safety and loving nurture of all family members."[1] Men and women are meant to be equal partners in this life. Elders represent the collective wisdom and experience of how to live on the land. Children are the best hope that the wisdom of the elders will continue. We must "Transmit to future generations values, traditions, and institutions that support the long-term flourishing of Earth's human and ecological communities."[2] When humans realize that we are all related, we can come to one mind on matters, build healthy relationships, and live healthy lives. By loving one another, we can assure that future generations will be born into the world where reason replaces violence.

Second, we are meant to share with one another. We look to the land as a huge bowl that provides life-giving foods and medicines so that human life can continue. We share one spoon to eat from that bowl. Each will take what he or she needs, not wasting what is left. Food and medicine do not belong to any one person. They were provided for the well-being of all. We should not be charging money for the gifts of nature, nor should we hoard the resources for our own. We need to respect the fact that food and medicine are sacred gifts of life, meant to be shared. As it says in the Earth Charter, we must "Accept that with the right to own, manage, and use natural resources comes the duty to prevent environmental harm and to protect the rights of people."[3] By sharing we teach cooperation and respect. By sharing, we "Care for the community of life with understanding, compassion, and love."[4] By sharing we all survive and human life can continue.

Third, humans have been asked to respect the life's breath that enters our bodies and allows us to exist. Life is a precious gift of time and we need to continually be thankful for what has been provided for us. All that is required for a happy and healthy life is already in front of us. As the Preamble of the Earth Charter says, a happy life "is primarily about being more, not having more."[5] We need to show respect for the sacred landscape in which we live. We need to "Respect Earth and life in all its diversity."[6] We need to respect ourselves and live in a peaceful and contributing way. Humans have a critical role in the well-being of the universe, and if we teach thoughts of love, sharing, and respect we can give the future generations not only hope, but also a way to fulfill that hope.

With that as a background, I find it difficult to express the full nature of the changes that have been brought to our land and people in the last five centuries. Nearly all that we believe about life has been exterminated, threatened, or suffers from lack of attention. It is a sad and troubling story to recall.

I will try to share some of my personal thoughts about our shared memories of the contact between our peoples. Some of the memories are great moments of love, sharing, and respect. Others are not so good. Too often the memory of the darker times can create a prison for our emotions, as we have inherited much historical grief.

Thinking of those values for human survival that I outlined, imagine what it must have been like the first time the Mohawk people heard the French guns blast their hot metal in 1609. French settlers, Samuel de Champlain, and some allied Native Americans attacked the Mohawks and after the smoke cleared, several lay dead, including three chiefs. The killing of the "men of peace" had a profound impact on the Haudenosaunee.

It is not that killing did not exist before. In fact, if the Haudenosaunee have one of the greatest traditions of peace, it is not because everyone was full of love, sharing, and respect. Just the opposite. Our people were caught in a seemingly endless cycle of hatred, violence, and war. Our Great Law of Peace brought that strife to an end when people remembered the values of the Original Instructions. By keeping the peace in mind, treating everyone with respect, and making sure that justice prevails, we can have what we call the Good Mind. We do this when we "Recognize that peace is the wholeness created by right relationships with oneself, other persons, other cultures, other life, Earth, and the larger whole of which all are a part."[7] Perhaps it is human nature to forget such things, especially when times are good. It takes hard work to keep the peace. It takes a strong mind to overcome heartache and tragedy.

My ancestors should have known better, but the lure of the fur trade and the desire for political and economic gain led them to take up arms against other Native American nations. The French, Dutch, and English were master manipulators. With their steel tomahawks and flint guns, the Haudenosaunee dominated native life in the Northeast. We forgot much of the Original Instructions and began to hack away at the sacred web of life. We settled for bright beads, shiny silver, and powerful weapons.

However, it was a short-lived "victory." Once the fur moved farther to the west and the Europeans were no longer in such fierce competition with one another, the Americans began to systematically remove the land from under the feet of my ancestors. We have all become aware of the dispossession of the Native Americans from their homelands. But think for a minute of what that dispossession must have done to the spirit of the people. Blood stained the ground where sacred ceremonies were once held. Great villages were turned into heaps of ash. Thousands of people were forced to flee into the uncertainty of the woods. Families became separated and lost. People were disconnected from the places where ancestors had practiced the Original Instructions. Their footprints were lost under wagon trails, train tracks, and sidewalks. The grandchildren became confused about where to go and what to do.

The same old story could be told of the hundreds of native nations of this land. As the zeal of Manifest Destiny swept from East to West, the Native Americans became the sacrificial lamb in the quest for spiritual unity in American culture. The irony of that fact is part of our collective memory. It still stings us to know that the romantic horizon of America's past is littered with the bones of our ancestors. The basic denial of our inalienable rights seems hard to fathom when we hear of religious freedom and the right to life, liberty, and the pursuit of happiness.

It is no wonder that some of our ancestors turned that oppression inward. A sad legacy of self-hatred was created, compounded of the experience of near extermination, displacement, and being sent off to schools that denied the validity of the ways of the ancestors. Our great-grandparents were taught to hate themselves because of their way of life. Even those who did not go to the boarding schools have inherited the dysfunction from a generation that did not see any family love, did not experience any community sharing, and had no models or respect. As tragic as massacres were, perhaps the more serious damage was done to the survivors. The cultures, beliefs, and values that had sustained their communities for centuries were replaced with a plow, a school bell, and a Bible.

For several generations the Native American survivors lived in virtual poverty, considered wards of the federal government. Our grandparents were not even considered capable of taking care of themselves. The sacred relationships of the past were severed. Reservations and Indian agencies were operated like prisons. It is amazing that any of our traditions survived at all. Children were taken away from their families, many to be adopted by non-Indians. Despite all this, the stories of the past were shared in the quiet moments, away from the eyes and ears of the jailers. Even though teachers would wash out our parents' mouths if they spoke their native languages, the people found a way to pass on their sacred memories about the old days—adding fresher memories of how their world had been turned upside down.

People my age grew up in a very different world from that experienced by our elders. Many of us were in denial about who we were and what we wanted out of life. We eked out a living from a family farm, making baskets, or getting a job in town. Our people still suffered from racism, bias, and oppression. There was not much hope in our communities. The federal and state governments continued to deny our political and human rights. Our lands were still under attack. We were reliving the experience of our ancestors, but it was the twentieth century. Things had not changed very much.

The time has come to break the cycle of ignorance, shame, and oppression. Many Native American communities have begun to heal themselves. Many good people are working hard to reclaim the values of love, sharing, and respect. The spirit of the people is reemerging. Everywhere I go I can see a renewal taking place. I can hear more Native American words of healing, comfort, and unity. I can hear more songs floating in the wind. People are dancing and celebrating life.

I try to do all I can to keep the values, beliefs, and way of life of my ancestors alive and thriving. The Earth Charter calls for us to "Affirm the right of indigenous peoples to their spirituality, knowledge, lands and resources" and upholds "the right of all, without discrimination, to a natural and social environment supportive of human dignity, bodily health, and spiritual well-being, with special attention to the rights of indigenous peoples. . . ."[8] I have traveled the world to spread the message of peace that we have inherited. I think it is profoundly important to continue the good dialogue started by our people many centuries ago when we would meet and polish the covenant chain of peace. We were really making relatives of each other. Some may call it a treaty making, but it was really making sure that we saw each other as relatives, just as the Original Instructions had told us.

Yet, there is still an important step to be taken. We have focused much attention on ourselves. We need to expand the circle of healing and begin a dialogue with other races, cultures, and belief systems. We have to find ways to overcome our hurt feelings and anger at the "white man." In order to be the kind of human beings envisioned at the time of creation, we need to overcome racial and cultural prejudices.

The Earth Charter can open the human eyes and the human heart to make this dialogue possible. The Earth Charter cannot replace the Original Instructions for Native Americans. It can, however, provide a larger framework within which we can have a dialogue with others about our sacred values. This dialogue will help us learn to walk again on our ancient and sacred path. The Original Instructions can inform the Earth Charter, too, helping others understand their own path.

NOTES

An earlier version of this essay was published as a Response to the Tap II Key Finding and Questions by the National Conference for Community and Justice in *Faith Leaders on Intergroup Relations: Perspectives and Challenges*, NCCJ Occasional Papers (2002). See <http://www.nccj.org/nccj/nccj.nsf/articleall/4538?opendocument&1#875>.

1. Earth Charter, Subprinciple 11c.
2. Earth Charter, Subprinciple 4b.
3. Earth Charter, Subprinciple 2a.
4. Earth Charter, Principle 2.
5. Earth Charter, Preamble, paragraph four.
6. Earth Charter, Principle 1.
7. Earth Charter, Subprinciple 16f.
8. Earth Charter, Subprinciple 12b and Principle 12.

Lake Conestee

John Lane

Dave Hargett's dream for Lake Conestee isn't really visible from the parking lot of the Racecar Speedy Mart. The impressive nineteenth-century stone dam on the Reedy River in Greenville, South Carolina, is in clear view though, and the boarded-up textile mill, closed twenty years ago, crowds in everyone's line of sight just off Conestee Road. To anyone driving past, the eighteen of us—two Wofford College professors, fifteen college students, and Dave—look a little suspicious, standing among the fire ant hills and stunted pines on the ridge above the river.

It's early fall and in only the minute or two we've stood with our fifteen freshmen looking out over the Reedy River we all consider beautiful, a great blue heron and red-tailed hawk have crossed paths low above what's left of the lake behind the dam. Appreciation of beauty in the natural world is easy to teach. Convincing these students that they are somehow responsible for understanding and even correcting the sort of environmental disaster that is contained in the story of Conestee is more difficult and will take far longer than an afternoon visit.

Dave is up for it though. He's sent us links to the Conestee Web site,[1] and with my colleague Ellen Goldey's expertise as a toxicologist we've sorted through pages of environmental history. Slender and dressed comfortably for the field in chinos and boots, Dave could just as easily be leading a bird walk as briefing a class on Conestee. He waves his arms and begins to tell us of the vision that has possessed a handful of people who have seen the potential here: a long corridor of greenway stretching along the Reedy River for twenty-five miles from Furman University all the way to this economically depressed community.

We've prepped our students for the Conestee field trip, told them that environmental visions in South Carolina have been few and far between. It's a state known more for a Bible Belt faith in "economic development," no matter what the cost. A few families (some local, some northeastern textile magnates) got rich off ventures like Conestee Mill, but the working people in the upstate have suffered mightily through two hundred years of industrial revolution—first the iron industry, then textiles, and now real estate speculation. Unlike the ruling class, the poor have little to show for their role in what former Supreme Court Chief Justice William Brennan once called "the war against the world." Wages have remained low and the old industrial communities—once thriving, though poor communities—were blighted when industries left, chasing even cheaper wages overseas.

The waterways of upstate South Carolina have shown the strain of "progress" maybe most of all. Nearly all the rivers and creeks in the region are classified as impaired by the South Carolina Department of Health and Environmental Control. All are unsafe to drink, and most aren't fit for swimming. Some still can't support aquatic life thirty-five years after the Clean Water Act was meant to put a stop to wholesale exploitation of these waterways for greed and profit and return them to fishable and swimmable conditions.

The discussion and this field trip are parts of two required general education courses, biology and humanities, linked around a theme, in this case, "The Nature and Culture of Water." In a former life Ellen worked as a researcher for the Environmental Protection Agency; she has a keen interest in toxins and has taught the students enough chemistry and fresh water ecology concerning the site to allow them to grasp its complexity as an industrial "brownfield." As a humanities professor I've spent class time talking about upstate environmental history, about issues of environmental justice and the complex set of values that allow a community to dam a river and then, in a little over a century, destroy the lake behind the dam.

Two of the students, Thomas and Amelia, took the linked classes as freshmen, and now they're back as sophomores to assist. They help the students grasp the material, give the linked courses continuity through their two-year participation, and shoulder the weighty titles of "preceptors." Today, their main role will be as kayak wranglers as we take the students out on the lake.

Dave, a local environmental scientist and activist, drives us behind the Speedy Mart and through a chain link fence to a launch site on the impoundment's east lobe. We unload our boats from the trailer—enough kayaks for us and the students and Dave's canoe—and Dave gathers us at the water and fills us in on the research to make the place real. He knows the history of this watery landscape, how in the 1940s, Lake Conestee (Cherokee for "land of beautiful water") was roughly 130 acres of open water, the dam and mill impoundment providing a power source for the mill since the 1830s. It was also a recreational centerpiece for the community and a source of supplementary protein for the workers—fish and turtles.

Now, aerial photos show a fifty-year-old river bottom forest maturing over thick sediment laid down by the Reedy during Greenville's busiest industrial decades. There's silt here from the clearing of the land for early agriculture, clay eroded off the Donaldson air base in the 1940s, the I-85 construction project of the late 1950s, and the industrial boom of the 1960s, all before there was any sediment control. And not only sediment came down the Reedy River channel to this first major dam below Greenville proper: core samples have shown there are also all the compounds used to create our current "standard of living"—lead, zinc, copper, and other heavy metals, PCBS, and pesticides in vast quantities, all "stored" here behind the thick Conestee mill dam.

The students take notes as Dave tells us about the vision for Conestee Park as we look back upstream toward the horizon line marking the spot where water courses down the old dam's face. What Dave sees when he looks toward the dam is the silted-in lake above, a place with navigable water and wildlife habitat. Working with the Conestee Foundation, the nonprofit that has purchased the lake, Dave envisions hiking and biking trails and an ecological education center on the three hundred acres of slough, island, shoreline, and mud flat near what he says will be the urban center of the city of Greenville in 2020.

We fit everybody in their kayaks. Thomas and Amelia go through a safety talk and check to make sure all the life jackets are snug and secure. These are stable lake kayaks, so we don't anticipate any trouble navigating the calm lake and river. Howard, a large basketball player, can't get his feet in his boat, so we switch him into a longer one. Amelia makes a joke about how if Howard's boat somehow sinks he can paddle one of his sneakers back to shore.

As we launch our boats, I wonder about the complex smells of this place: peat or sewage? Somewhere below in the sediment is what Dave calls "black mayonnaise," a layer of sludge laid down since 1892, years before Greenville treated the discharge from its sewage plant positioned a few miles upstream. This shit savannah, this delta of deadly compounds, holds all the sins of the industrial upstate, washed downstream and deposited like sand where the current slowed behind the Conestee dam. As we paddle upstream I learn, once again, that we're all downstream from something, somebody.

On the water it's like paddling in Africa, not upstate South Carolina. The Conestee sloughs open up into bays fringed by yellow water primrose and a backdrop of mature oaks and poplars. Dave points out that the water primrose, though beautiful, is not native. It's an intrusive weed species. Ellen agrees, but notes that it's hiding all the Conestee trash—cans, Styrofoam, bottles, balls of every sort: football, soccer, basketball, anything that will float.

We cruise around the bay, and I'm baffled by how much something can change in my mind from ugly to beautiful by just cruising into the middle of it. From shore this old silted-in industrial reservoir looks like a wasteland, not a wonderland, or "oasis," as Dave keeps calling it. Then there is a whistle of a red-tailed hawk upset as we cruise close to where a nest is hidden. The bird's call brings me back to Dave's dreams. I hear something and turn—a turtle big as an old black skillet lumbers down off the bank into the water.

After the hawks have fallen silent, we portage over a narrow strand of hardwoods like early explorers, dragging our boats from the bay where we put in to an old river channel and paddle upstream. Birds everywhere! They seem not to mind the sewage sludge below, though tissue samples from fish this summer will show more of what we can't see, hope isn't happening. Ellen gathers everyone together and reminds them that we're hiking over what the toxicologists call "biomagnification," concentrations of contaminants, all the way up the food chain, a little Rachel Carson nightmare, right here in our own backyard. The bird life is abundant: little green herons, great blue herons, cormorants, all eating fish. Dozens of "woodies," the wood ducks whose boxes rise upward every few hundred yards of shoreline, cruising these waters and grazing the duckweed. Along the shore are the ones we can't see: tracks of deer, raccoon. Dave tells me stories of seeing otters swimming in these waters.

We land the boats, gather the group, bushwhack a few yards, and hit a well-traveled four-wheeler trail traversing an island in the old lake's north corner. There are red flags through the woods, signs of an archeological survey showing that Archaic and Woodlands peoples lived here thousands of years ago, working quartz and imported chert, making pottery, hauling in soapstone from quarries in the upstate. This high spot on the island is where Dave hopes to put some sort of structure for environmental education, high above the wetlands and the river. I look around and note the loveliness of these neglected woods. Full summer's green expanse closes in around us.

Back on the river Thomas, leading the way in his kayak, follows a pair of wood ducks. Some of us get close enough to see the way they drag one wing in the water, faking injury to draw us away from their young ones, hiding in the mats of flowers. So much life here! These cycles go on—birth, the raising of the young. And what of our young? Why have so few seen wood ducks perform to protect a summer's brood? "One hundred thousand school children are within a thirty-minute bus ride of this place," Dave says.

I look back at our line of kayaks strung out along the Reedy River. We are like a flock of brightly colored water birds following Dave in his green canoe. Headed back to the launch site, we slosh through the flowers and mud to cut through to the bay we started in. We slide our boats behind us, and several of us sink knee-deep into the sludge.

The week before we'd introduced the class to the Earth Charter, several dozen panels of cascading pledges packed onto a teal and white tri-fold brochure. We told them this charter was the result of years of negotiation among a wide variety of people and organizations and nations to articulate the complexity of a world environmental vision. "We stand at a critical moment in Earth's history," the Earth Charter states in the Preamble, "a time when humanity must choose its future."[2]

The summer before Ellen and I had been two of a group of a hundred academics in Chewonki, Maine. We were professors, administrators, college presidents, gathered to talk about the Earth Charter. Our goal was what conference organizer Peter Blaze Corcoran called "the urgency of moving higher education toward sustainability."

On the first night Thomas Berry and Steven C. Rockefeller were keynote speakers. Rockefeller spoke first as introduction. As one of the key architects of the Earth Charter, he described the charter as "the most negotiated document in human history."

Ecotheologian Thomas Berry stood up to speak next. He's an old soul, hunched, closing in on his ninetieth year. In his clear voice he brought his idea of "the Great Work" into the room. It's been his lifework, a search for a planetary ethic. Above us that night hung the imposing skeleton of a Fin whale killed by a freighter off the coast of Virginia. "When we are all gone, the memory I will have is of the whale," Berry said, "the guardian spirit and presence." He described creation as "a communion of subjects rather than a collection of objects," a perspective necessary for the "long-term flourishing of the earth's human and ecological communities."

Later in the week Bucknell University professor of religion and ecology Mary Evelyn Tucker called the Earth Charter "a song of hope" and stated that "we need to hear, play and dance to that music." She explained how the Earth Charter could be used possibly as "soft law," like an "international declaration of planetary rights." Or it could be used as an educational tool if a conference like the one at Chewonki was successful. As she explained it, the Earth Charter pulled together many concerns and common hopes.

From that Maine conference we brought back our own set of hopes—that our students would see the importance of not only thinking critically about environmental issues. We wanted them to feel deeply as well. We wanted them to fall in love with our abused neglected Piedmont landscape. So with our students we discussed how difficult it is to find common ground among all the world's citizens, and now in this place I think of Thomas Berry and his book *The Dream of the Earth*: "We are returning to our native place after a long absence, meeting once again with our kin in the earth community."[3] I remind myself that the promise of the Earth Charter and Thomas Berry's earth community includes these wood ducks and the hawks as great citizens of this watery commonwealth. These dreams even include the bacteria working at the sludge below the lake's neglected surface.

As we land our boats I hear the water over the Conestee dam just downstream, see the top of the old abandoned cotton mill. There is so much beauty here, but also so much uncertainty about what is under the surface. That's the ugliness—what we don't know, what we can't afford to clean up. I take one last look at Lake Conestee before loading the boats on the trailer. It's as if the whole long history of our exploitation of the Piedmont is contained here in these images, these sounds. It will take decades of deep earth dreams to restore Conestee to a vision of wholeness, but those who have learned to love the lake seem up to it. We'll return here each year and float these sloughs and listen for the red-tail's whistle.

NOTES

1. The Conestee Web site is www.upstateforever.org/programs_conestee.html.

2. Earth Charter, Preamble, paragraph one.

3. Berry, Thomas. *The Dream of the Earth*. San Francisco: Sierra Club Books, 1988, 1.

Restoration
A Plan

Rick Bass

I despair often, when I consider the challenges we face in attempting not just to hold the line on our ever-diminishing American wilderness, but to restore some of the elements—almost ghosts, now—that are so critical to the spirit and function of that wildness. The grizzly bear that feeds upon and then disperses in its scat the seed caches of whitebark pine, stored in mounds along the windiest, most remote ridgetops by the raucous-shouting Clark's nutcrackers. The black-backed woodpeckers hammering on the drums of the remaining spars of burned and "unsalvaged" lodgepole in remote forests, swarming the dead and dying wood, feeding upon the insects that helped birth and perpetuate this portion of the forest's cycle.

Butterflies, blue sulphurs and gingham checkers, drifting through the firescape, and bluebirds like blazes of neon, or blazes and patches of sky, hurtling through the burned forest, and mushrooms leaping from the ash—always, in a rich and diverse landscape, the presence of one thing not only accommodates its opposite, but is often reliant upon that opposite. It is a healthy, vibrant tolerance.

In the valley where I live—the Yaak, on the Kootenai National Forest, in extreme northwestern Montana—nothing has yet gone extinct, not since the Ice Age, at any rate. Many species are down to single-digit populations, as if in a reverse kind of Noah's ark; but they're all still here, hanging on.

Things are still connected in the wild Yaak, and a few other crumbs of wild places in the Lower 48, and I am convinced that when each of a landscape's time-crafted species is still present in a place, there emanates a vitality, a spirit, that is larger than the sum of even all those amazing parts: a magic, or what seems to us like magic, but is perhaps simply the condition that once existed everywhere.

Evidence of our growing awareness of the need to preserve such places as the Yaak, to bring them back to their full vitality, can be found in a document such as the Earth Charter. While intended as a set of guiding principles for the new global environment, the Earth Charter can assist us in becoming grounded in our local places. The Earth Charter states in the Preamble that "The resilience of the community of life and the well-being of humanity depend upon preserving a healthy biosphere with all its ecological systems, a rich variety of plants and animals, fertile soils, pure waters, and clean air."[1] And forests like those in the Yaak, with magic in their wildness, and their health.

"Magic" is not a particularly easy word to use. It can be vague and abstract, soft and nebulous. Generations of suspicious nondialogue between environmentalists and resource extraction representatives have had the terms of these nondialogues defined not by environmentalists nor by any alliance of common ground, but rather, solely by industry.

Chief among the myths that have emerged from such nondialogue is the myth that logging prevents fire, and the myth that we could begin logging at one end of the Yaak and work our way to the other end, and that by the time we got to the other side, a wild forest would have grown up behind us, more vibrant and diverse than ever.

Worst of all is the myth that an ancient forest is unnatural, in sore need of our manipulation, our fractional knowledge, our cultivation. That it cannot survive in a healthful condition without our monitoring and attendance. That it cannot survive unless we build roads into it and log it, pulp it and peel it and shred and cube it, and then replant those tractor-crushed hardpan soils with our own fast growing spindly seedlings from nurseries in orchard-row fashion.

In the Pacific Northwest, and in the corner of northwestern Montana that falls under its shadow, our appetites have indeed been prodigious. The Kootenai National Forest—with the Yaak in its heart—has produced more timber than any other valley in Montana, year after year after year. Some years it produces up to half the state's total volume of federal timber—the bulk of it coming from one tiny island.

In such a culture, where, unless one gets up in an airplane, it's hard to see how few really big trees are left, it's sometimes hard to speak out on behalf of salamanders, or butterflies, or ferns, or even grizzlies. (Elk, sometimes, you can talk about, because they're "useful"—they're thrilling to hunt, and delicious, and somehow manly; but conversations regarding the other things have not found much purchase here.)

But such inaudible conversations have been growing nonetheless, silently, and at depth.

The conversations—all right, I'll say it, the arguments—when we've been fortunate enough to have them—have traditionally focused on volume and fiber and tonnage and economics, on legalities and policy. On how to get more, take more, one last time.

We need desperately, I think, a story—even a myth, or a dream, or a plan, for the time being—of restoration.

Best of all, I think, would be a story that doesn't waste too much time looking back casting blame upon the past, and its abuses and corruption and plain old-fashioned mistakes and misinformation. It would be easy to do nothing but criticize the rogue past of the Kootenai, and the selfish interests of the corporations that have passed through these parts, liquidating their own private lands, and then liquidating the Kootenai, if they could.

How many second chances will we get? How many chances will we get—in the words of the Earth Charter—to "Internalize the full environmental and social costs of goods and services in the selling price, and enable consumers to identify products that meet the highest social and environmental standards"?[2] Or to "Adopt lifestyles that emphasize the quality of life and material sufficiency in a finite world"?[3] Maybe I'm pessimistic, but all I can see from where I stand is one more chance. But if we do it right, or as close to right as we can, isn't that enough?

The story has so far almost always been the same, and with the same results, ever-diminishing to our power and dignity and self-respect; and still, like moths to a flame, we rise again and again to industry's saber rattling, and join in with industry's cries for less government regulations on these poor hard-working corporations. In Montana, one recent ex-governor cried that she intended to be "the lapdog of industry" for these corporations: Boise Cascade, Champion International, Sterling Mining, Plum Creek Limited, Asarco Mining, and W. R. Grace, to name only a few.

And from these rural pockets, decade after decade, even after industry has plunged its dagger into their heart, the saber rattlers bleat about the perceived rights and privileges that industry has convinced them are their due, even as on the matters of responsibility and accountability, they are silent.

And even as they—the one-horse company towns, and the polarized, frightened communities these companies have agitated time and time again—poison the air or pollute the water or replace our old forests with fields of weeds, and our bugling elk with silence, and our grizzlies with nothing—we fight among ourselves, like scarab beetles in a jar.

Always, the story is the same. If it is a mining company, they post a tiny clean-up bond, generally one-tenth of what ends up being required to do a full clean-up after they're gone. They claw the ore out from beneath the mountains, leaching the gold with cyanide, or blasting the copper out with dynamite, hauling the silver away and leaving in the creeks and rivers poisonous levels of lead and mercury. And when the state or federal government asks them to clean up the mess—always, with mining, there is poison—the mining company instead files for bankruptcy, disassembles its board of directors, moves to another state, reassembles the same board of directors (who have been chosen for their political connections), and with a new parent company begins the same process all over again, while in their wake, the taxpayers are stuck with the multimillion-dollar reclamation bills, as well as the enduring legacy of toxins.

With the timber companies, the story is always the same. They take the biggest and best trees from the public lands while leaving behind the ones that truly do need thinning, either by fire or by saw. They bilk the taxpayer into building expensive logging roads far into the national forests, and they clearcut any private land they might own in the area, too. They put their profits into labor-saving technology, rather than paying higher wages to the workers, and lay off more workers even as they run more and more timber through the mill.

They blame the environmentalists, even during a glut of cheap or unsellable timber, and when transport costs or energy costs or insurance premiums or foreign competition or a construction industry downturn puts them out of business, they move to the Southeast, where trees grow twice as fast, and where their product is closer to a more vibrant construction industry and various seaports.

But before they leave town they convert their good old-fashioned sawmill/timber company into a limited partnership real estate investment trust, so that they don't have to pay taxes beyond a certain minimal cap; and of those taxes, they pay them on a much lower agricultural land classification, rather than as the prime real estate their land has suddenly become. They divide a wild landscape into five-acre tracts, and leave.

And still, we ask for more "local control," and for ever-lessening restrictions on the way these companies do business on our nation's public lands, and in our local communities.

With the hydroelectricity projects, the story is also always the same. They tell us we can have it all—cheap power, clean power, and salmon, sturgeon, wild trout, flood control and irrigation—all of it, if only we'll build one more dam on one last wild river. Pacific Power and Light told us this, most recently, asking only that we deregulate them, which our state's Republican super-majority was only too glad to do. (The previous quarter's earnings for PP&L went up 900 percent, power prices were expected to escalate 400 percent the next autumn, and with stream flows in the Northwest at twenty-three percent of average, if you think the needs of wild salmon are going to be given any consideration, you can think again. . . .)

All of these stories began well over a hundred years ago, and they just keep playing themselves out, over and over again. The Earth Charter, as has been noted increasingly by others as well, connects the role of unfettered development to the degradation of our local communities: "The dominant patterns of production and consumption are causing environmental devastation, the depletion of resources, and a massive extinction of species. Communities are being undermined."[4] Yet the same stories persist. Right or wrong, a story can last almost forever.

Isn't this all really just a bunch of tattling? Placater and peacemaker that I am, all I really want to do is just walk off into the wilderness and find a place of quiet peace. Isn't this all just a bunch of tiresome tattling, without a solution, a plan? Do we really need any narrative to tell us, for example, that W. R. Grace mined asbestos right outside of the town of Libby, releasing deadly tremolite fibers into the air by the ton, for years after company and perhaps state officials knew these fibers caused an incurable kind of lung cancer? Do we really need the statistics, the preliminary screenings that show up to a third of the population of that town have evidence of some degree of pleural thickening, perhaps indicative of the beginning stages of the disease?

Always, the story is the same, and yet always, we return to these pleas and promises; we pursue and implore these companies to come into our forest, to come into our town, and we lobby on their behalf. They say the words we want them to say, and they tell us, again and again, that they will take care of us, and that the government is our enemy; that boundaries and guidelines and rules and protections are our enemy. They praise our native spunk and grit and then they take everything we have and pour poison into us and upon our land, and then they leave. And they leave in their wake perhaps the worst thing of all: an embittered and polarized culture, in which generations of fierce intolerance have resulted in a culture in which imagination is no longer always seen as the form of boldness and empowerment that it can be, but instead as a weakness and a danger—a fey and useless thing, to be ridiculed, criticized, denigrated. Stop dreaming those dreams. There's one more cache of ore to cut, one more roadless area to enter. Get out of the way.

Surely the beginning of any new dream or plan must have as its foundation the security of all of our last remaining roadless areas: the last crumbs, the tattered archipelago of baseline health: the little cells that still contain the essence of that breath of wilderness that future generations stand at risk of forgetting, or, worse yet, never knowing.

I hate using numbers to describe this roadless base—I want to use words, images, and the senses—but the numbers tell a story, too. The roadless areas of our national forests contain only two-tenths of one percent of our nation's timber supply, and the market is glutted, and yet still industry clamors for these last sacred lands. How can a solution be found, with such a partner, such a combatant? Why must we always fight, and over such crumbs?

All right, then: enough caterwauling. In crisis there is opportunity. Our grizzlies are vanishing, our clearcuts are filling in with knapweed, dandelions, rush skeletonweed, toadflax, and worst of all, the hideously unstoppable orange hawkweed; our native trout are hanging on, but under siege, as is almost every other rare and delicate species, be it owl or mammal or tender orchid. The Yaak, with its back up against the wall of Canada, survived—just barely—the onslaught of the last century, but can it survive the next? Or rather, can its wildness survive?

Because the Kootenai—particularly the upper reaches, which include the Yaak—has been degraded more than any other valley in Montana, it is here where we should first focus our efforts on restoration, as well as conservation. The Earth Charter states that we should "Promote the recovery of endangered species and ecosystems."[5] For decades, the Yaak has given, and given, and given; if there is to be any grace and balance to the story, any valid recovery, it should begin with this acknowledgment: that it is the time to report the excesses of the past.

The forest in the Yaak has been turned upside down; could not have become more inverted than had the hand of a troublesome giant lifted it from these mountains and flipped it over. In a landscape that once might have been as much as fifty percent old growth, over two-thirds of our forest is now comprised of trees that measure seventeen inches or less in diameter at chest height, which is a very small tree indeed. This "overstock" is the result of two main factors, the clearcuts of the past—in whose scabrous wakes have rushed a tangle of young trees all of the same age—and totalitarian fire suppression efforts of the past.

By now we realize and understand the basics of fire ecology: that if more fires had been allowed to burn, they would have helped clean out the historic build-up of twigs and leaves and needles that carry the fires so rapidly, and would have thinned out a lot of those overstocked seedlings and saplings, and stimulated growth.

You'll be hearing from the timber industry that logging can simulate the low-intensity wildfires we've been lacking. And like most such claims by either industry or environmentalists, in some places, under some circumstances, they're right—hypothetically, at least. What industry's not telling you, though, is that it costs money to do that kind of logging—taking the fine fuels and poles and saplings, while leaving the larger trees, which would have historically been spared anyway by the more frequent, low-intensity fires that we used to have commonly.

Instead, with many of the current timber prescriptions, industry goes into a forest and whacks about half of the mature green trees, leaving half, so that the result is more aesthetic than the clearcuts of the past; but they still haven't addressed those twigs and branches, the ignition sources—the choking detritus that is the true fuel hazard, far more so than the mature green trees themselves.

It's extremely expensive to go in and slash and pile all those overstocked saplings by hand, in what's called a "mechanical treatment," and that's all right, I suppose. It's job creating, though, and fulfills a need, and provides a service of value, so that I have no qualms about paying for that service, as long as it takes place out of those last fourteen roadless areas—those baseline reference points of forest health and diversity and wildness. And there are places—particularly along the interfaces between private and public land, in the West—where the higher-priced mechanical treatment is probably wisest and safest.

With prescribed burns, you can treat seven times as much landscape for the same amount of money, and in a far more beneficial manner, leaving the forest's nutrients on-site.

And on the Kootenai, particularly—Montana's wettest forest, the closest thing our state has to a rainforest, particularly in these days of global warming—we can burn "better," which is to say at a lower, steadier intensity, and with more predictability of direction, than anywhere else in the state.

It's things like these that make me think the Kootenai, more than any forest in the National Forest System, is the ideal and obvious candidate to be treated as a Conservation and Restoration National Forest: a national forest that, in that naming, would receive acknowledgment that it is a unique and valuable landscape, and one to which restoration is long overdue. Not a charter or community forest, siphoned out of the public treasury, but on the contrary: cherished, retained in the public safekeeping, and restored, in partnership between expert Forest Service personnel and communities.

Clever as our engineers are, not in a million years could we go out and buy, or design, or fashion, much less construct such a landscape as this one, not even on a garden-scale fraction of what we've still got here, in the Yaak.

The advantages for such a designation and management are immediately obvious. It's important to remember that each year as a nation we spend millions on the protection of endangered species, as required by the Endangered Species Act, a giant piece of conservation legislation passed by the Nixon administration in 1974.

On the Kootenai, in addition to possessing an ever-increasing list of threatened and endangered species—our small clan of super-survivor grizzlies, their unique low-elevation genes as good as gold, crafted as they are to these shady interior forests; our occasional woodland caribou, our wolves and eagles and bull trout and sturgeon, our falcons and water howellia—we have an even longer (and increasing) list of sensitive species that have been pushed to the brink: great gray owls, Coeur d'Alene salamanders, westslope cutthroat trout, pure inland redband trout, shorthead sculpin, to name only a few. There are easily a hundred more—lynx, wolverine, northern bog lemming, and on and on. . . .

In the Kootenai, we come face to face, palpably, with the Earth Charter notion that "all beings are interdependent and every form of life has value regardless of its worth to human beings."[6]

How much more efficient, how much more fiscally conservative, to lay down a long-term plan designed for the benefit of this vast interconnected and interdependent matrix, this underpinning biotic structure that helps comprise the spirit of this place.

The Kootenai didn't even earn a profit back in the heyday of high-volume high-grade clearcutting. Why not turn toward restoration? Why not nurture—incubate—a local wood-processing facility that takes what the Kootenai has to give, for once, rather than dictating (in terms of big green mature fire-resistant timber) what we want the answer to be, regardless of sustainability?

Make no mistake: such a program would create more and newer jobs. Heavy equipment operators would be needed, more than ever, to repair or obliterate the damaged roads that are pouring sediment into our fisheries, and the sawyers would need to thin the unnatural and unhealthy build-up of fine fuels. Field workers need to monitor stream flows and temperatures, and plant and animal populations.

The nature of all these jobs—unlike those of the past—is sustainable.

In the wake of the excesses of the past, there are so many opportunities for this kind of work—and this kind of forestry—on the Kootenai. We need to begin aggressively reconnecting our last little pockets of ancient forests, too, particularly the old mature larch, which is the rarest form of old growth in the West, and yet the most common in the Yaak. I'd like to envision a Big Larch Reserve, stunning gold in the autumn, with mammoth trees such as the ones that used to stud almost half of the entire valley, widely spaced and—I'll use that word again, unapologetically—magical. With only a hundred years of recovery, it might be possible one day for a traveler to walk through a band of such a forest stretching miles wide, all the way up into Canada, where such a reserve is already protected. (By "reserve," I do not necessarily mean no cutting—on the contrary, in places, burning and mechanical treatment, winter logging, might be needed to enhance the release of the desired condition of big larch, and lots of them.)

Over seventy percent of the American public wants our public wildlands, our last roadless lands, protected from any kind of logging. A handful of people in the 110th Congress and George W. Bush's administration do not want these lands protected; but if seventy percent of a nation is to be bullied by a handful of the special-interest suck-egg corporations, then shame on us, and on all our hollow talk of freedom and democracy, and rights and responsibilities.

I'm convinced that in this day and age an environmentalist's dreams and plans are nearly as vital an underpinning and latticework of wild habitat as are the mountains and rivers and forests themselves. Once upon a time, it used not to be this way, but now, paradoxically, in these desperate days, dreams and big ideas are absolutely critical. Politics, activism, and desire have become their own kind of required habitat for a region, in these last days.

And yet it's true, too, that dreams are only half of what's required. The muscle of activism, the dreadful grunt-work, is the other half, and at least as important. The Earth Charter reminds us that the renewal we seek will take "a change of mind and heart. It requires a new sense of global interdependence and universal responsibility. We must imaginatively develop and apply the vision of a sustainable way of life locally, nationally, regionally, and globally."[7]

In an age in which the wilderness is becoming less and less visible, it seems odd that one of the things most required to keep it alive, or to bring it back, is also the unseen—the passion of the people to whom the wilderness is beloved: loggers, hunters, anglers, hikers, environmentalists, schoolteachers, schoolchildren, businesspeople—almost everyone. We must find ways, as the Earth Charter concludes, "to harmonize diversity with unity, the exercise of freedom with the common good, short-term objectives with long-term goals. Every individual, family, organization, and community has a vital role to play."[8]

Unseen, then, those dreams, but not unspoken. Not on the Kootenai, at least. There is still barely time to protect and retain that which is rare and vital and magic. There is still barely time to dream a new story. And then to act.

NOTES

1. Earth Charter, Preamble, paragraph two.
2. Earth Charter, Subprinciple 7d.
3. Earth Charter, Subprinciple 7f.

4. Earth Charter, Preamble, paragraph three.
5. Earth Charter, Subprinciple 5c.
6. Earth Charter, Subprinciple 1a.
7. Earth Charter, The Way Forward, paragraph two.
8. Earth Charter, The Way Forward, paragraph three.

Wilderness as a Sabbath for the Land

Scott Russell Sanders

If you honor the sabbath in any way, or if you respect the beliefs of those who do, or if you merely suspect there may be some wisdom bound up in this ancient practice, then you should protect wilderness. For wilderness represents in space what the sabbath represents in time—a limit to our dominion, a refuge from the quest for power and wealth, an acknowledgment that Earth does not belong to us.

In scriptures that have inspired Christians, Muslims, and Jews, we are told to remember the sabbath and keep it holy by making it a day of rest for ourselves, our servants, our animals, and the land. This is a day free from the tyranny of getting and spending, a day given over to the cultivation of spirit rather than the domination of matter. During the remainder of the week, busy imposing our will on things, we may mistake ourselves for gods. But on the sabbath we recall that we are not the owners or rulers of this magnificent planet. Each of us receives life as a gift, and each of us depends for sustenance on the whole universe, the soil and water and sky and everything that breathes. The sabbath is yet another gift to us, a respite from toil, and also a gift to Earth, which needs relief from our appetites and ambitions.

Honoring the sabbath means to leave a portion of time unexploited, to relinquish for a spell our moneymaking, our striving, our designs. Honoring wilderness means to leave a portion of space unexploited, to leave the minerals untapped, the soils unplowed, the trees uncut, and to leave unharmed the creatures that live there. Both wilderness and sabbath teach us humility and restraint. They call us back from our ingenious machines and our thousand schemes to dwell with full awareness in the glory of the given world. By putting us in touch with the source of things, they give us a taste of paradise.

The instruction to honor the sabbath appears as the fourth of the commandments announced by Moses after his descent from Mount Sinai, as reported in the Book of Exodus in the Hebrew Bible:

> Remember the sabbath day, and keep it holy. Six days you shall labor and do all your work. But the seventh day is a sabbath to the Lord your God; you shall not do any work—you, your son or your daughter, your male or female slave, your livestock, or the alien resident in your towns. For in six days the Lord made heaven and earth, the sea, and all that is in them, but rested the seventh day; therefore the Lord blessed the sabbath day and consecrated it. (Ex. 20:8–11; all biblical quotations from the New Revised Standard Version)

If the Lord quit shaping Earth after six days, looked at what had been made, and saw that it was very good—as chronicled in the Book of Genesis—then who are we to keep reshaping Earth all seven days? On the sabbath we are to lay down our tools, cease our labors, set aside our plans, so that we may enjoy the sweetness of *being* without *doing*. On this holy day, instead of struggling to subdue the world, we are to savor it, praise it, wonder over it, and commune with the Creator who brought the entire world into existence.

The Book of Deuteronomy provides another reason for resting on the sabbath: "Remember that you were a slave in the land of Egypt, and the Lord your God brought you out from there with a mighty hand and an outstretched arm; therefore the Lord your God commanded you to keep the sabbath day" (Deut. 5:12–15). By reminding the Hebrew people of their own liberation from bondage, the sabbath calls on them to reenact that liberation every seventh day for the benefit of everyone and everything under their control.

Observing the sabbath would not always have been easy for a farming people, as one can sense from another version of the commandment: "Six days you shall work, but on the seventh day you shall rest; even in plowing time and in harvest time you shall rest" (Ex. 34:21). A delay in plowing or harvesting might mean the difference between a good crop and a poor one, so this was a severe discipline indeed. When I was a boy in rural Ohio some fifty years ago, I knew farmers who would not start a machine or harness a horse on the sabbath, no matter the weather or the state of their crops. Nor would they take up saws or scythes to work by hand. The most they would do was walk the fields, scooping up handfuls of soil, inspecting corn or hay, listening for birds, all as a way of gauging the health of their place.

The link between honoring the sabbath and honoring the Earth is spelled out elsewhere in Exodus:

> For six years you shall sow your land and gather in its yield; but the seventh year you shall let it rest and lie fallow, so that the poor of your people may eat; and what they leave the wild animals may eat. You shall do the same with your vineyard, and with your olive orchard. Six days you shall do your work, but on the seventh day you shall rest, so that your ox and your donkey may have relief, and your homeborn slave and the resident alien may be refreshed. (Ex. 23:10–12)

The great gift of the sabbath is refreshment, renewal, a return to the state of wholeness. It is medicine for soil and spirit, a healing balm.

After every seventh year of rest for the Earth, according to the Book of Leviticus, the people of Israel were to celebrate the fiftieth year as a jubilee, when the land must be left fallow, all debts must be forgiven, all slaves and indentured servants must be freed, and all property must be returned to its original owners. "The land shall not be sold in perpetuity," God proclaims, "for the land is mine; with me you are but aliens and tenants" (Lev. 25:23). This insistence that Earth belongs to God, not to humankind, echoes through the Bible, as in Psalm 24, which begins, "The earth is the Lord's and all that is in it, the world, and those who live in it; for he has founded it on the seas, and established it on the rivers" (Ps. 24:1–2); or in Psalm 50, where God says, "I will not accept a bull from your house, or goats from your folds. For every wild animal of the forest is mine, the cattle on a thousand hills. I know all the birds of the air, and all that moves in the field is mine. If I were hungry, I would not tell you, for the world and all that is in it is mine" (Ps. 50:9–12).

Whether celebrated every fiftieth year, every seventh year, or every seventh day, the sabbath links an obligation to care for the poor—the great theme of Jesus and the Hebrew prophets—with an obligation to care for the land and all the creatures that depend on the land for shelter and food.

According to a pair of stories in the Gospel of Luke, Jesus embraced the liberating power of the sabbath. Once Jesus was teaching in a synagogue on the sabbath when "there appeared a woman with a spirit that had crippled her for eighteen years. She was bent over and was quite unable to stand up straight." Jesus spoke to her and laid his hands on her, whereupon "she stood up straight and began praising God." When the Pharisees took him to task for healing on the day of rest, Jesus replied, "Does not each of you on the sabbath untie his ox or his donkey from the manger, and lead it away to give it water? And ought not this woman, a daughter of Abraham whom Satan bound for eighteen long years, be set free from this bondage on the sabbath day?" (Luke 13:10–16). On another occasion, after curing a man of dropsy on the sabbath, Jesus defended his action by asking the Pharisees, "If one of you has a child or an ox that has fallen into a well, will you not immediately pull it out on a sabbath day?" (Luke 14:5).

In both stories, Jesus interpreted the sabbath as a day for the breaking of fetters. Instead of dwelling on what was forbidden, he dwelt on what was required—the relief of suffering, the restoration of health. The Gospel of Mark tells of another sabbath when the Pharisees challenged Jesus for allowing his disciples to pluck heads of grain to relieve their hunger:

> And he said to them, "Have you never read what David did when he and his companions were hungry and in need of food? He entered the house of God, when Abiathar was high priest, and ate the bread of the Presence, which it is not lawful for any but the priests to eat, and he gave some to his companions." Then he said to them, "The sabbath was made for humankind, and not humankind for the sabbath." (Mark 2:25–27)

In that rousing last line, Jesus may seem to be turning the commandment on its head, yet he is actually recalling the spirit of freedom and jubilee implicit in the gift of the sabbath. In his reading, the sabbath becomes a foretaste of the kingdom of God, which is founded on compassion. Just as the universe, Earth, and all living things arise out of the great unfolding of God, so the sabbath is a reminder of this marvelous generosity. It is a day for deliverance not merely from toil but from whatever entraps us.

Our traps may be physical, as in the case of disease, but they may also be social or psychological. We may be trapped by poverty or by the relentless pursuit of wealth. We may be trapped by hatred or fear, by duties or lust. We may be trapped by the delusion that the world exists to satisfy our cravings. We may be trapped by addiction to chemicals or gadgets or noise. From all of these snares, and more, the sabbath can help to release us.

And yet for most Americans, even those who attend church or synagogue or mosque, in recent decades the sabbath has lost much of its serenity and nearly all of its meaning. Instead of being a day set aside for reflection and renewal, it has become a time for shopping, for catching up on chores, for watching television or movies, for mowing lawns or waxing cars, for burning up gas on the highways, for eating out or sleeping in. More and more jobs keep people on duty through the weekend. More and more stores, like the Internet, never close. Commerce and its minion, advertising, have spread around the clock, leaving scarcely any stretch of time unclaimed. In the same way, our machines and pollution have spread nearly everywhere on land and sea, leaving scarcely any stretch of Earth unclaimed.

This onslaught is squeezing out the wildness from our hearts and minds, as well as from the planet. The first word of the sabbath commandment is *remember*—remember to rest, to limit your schemes, to relieve from toil all who depend on you. Remember that you were a slave and have been set free; remember that life itself is a gift from God; remember that Earth and its abundance belong to the Lord. Instead of remembering, we are quickly forgetting who we are, where we are, and how we ought to live.

Although widely neglected, the practice of honoring the sabbath is a powerful example of "the traditional knowledge and spiritual wisdom in all cultures that contribute to environmental protection and human well-being."[1] Consider how many elements of the Earth Charter are implicit in the sabbath instructions. Granting "relief" on the seventh day to oxen, donkeys, and other livestock serves to "Prevent cruelty to animals kept in human societies and protect them from suffering," not merely by offering them water and rest, but also by reminding owners that these are fellow sentient creatures.[2] The requirement that slaves, too, be granted a respite so that they may be "refreshed" has a similar effect. The sabbath rules take for granted the institution of slavery, yet by insisting on the needs even of human chattels, they invite masters to "Recognize the ignored, protect the vulnerable, [and] serve those who suffer."[3] By proposing the liberation of slaves, the release of indentured servants, and the redistribution of property, the fiftieth-year jubilee constitutes an even more radical demand for equity, including "the equitable distribution of wealth."[4]

The principle of caring for those most in need is also embodied in the command to let the fields, olive orchards, and vineyards remain fallow every seventh year, "so that the poor of your people may eat; and what they leave the wild animals may eat" (Ex. 23:11). The inclusion of animals, both wild and tame, in the gift of the sabbath is consistent with the claim that "all beings are interdependent and every form of life has value regardless of its worth to human beings."[5] Land that is periodically allowed to remain fallow will be far more likely to preserve its fertility, a goal in keeping with the Earth Charter's call to "Manage the use of renewable resources such as water, soil, forest products, and marine life in ways that do not exceed rates of regeneration and that protect the health of ecosystems."[6] Insofar as a society takes care to avoid exhausting the soil or any other natural gifts, it acknowledges "that the freedom of action of each generation is qualified by the needs of future generations."[7]

If one accepts the argument that protecting wilderness represents in space what honoring the sabbath represents in time—a limit to our dominion, a curb on our getting and spending—then other principles of the Earth Charter come into play, such as the call to "Establish and safeguard viable nature and biosphere reserves, including wild lands and marine areas, to protect Earth's life support systems, maintain biodiversity, and preserve our natural heritage."[8] One such biosphere reserve, the Arctic National Wildlife Refuge in Alaska, is home not only to caribou, polar bears, muskoxen, wolverines, wolves, golden eagles, snow geese, and some 150 other species of birds, but also to the Gwich'in Indians, whose name means People of the Caribou, and who depend on this area for their subsistence way of life. Therefore, keeping oil derricks and other industrial activity out of the Arctic Refuge is a way of affirming "the right of indigenous peoples to their spirituality, knowledge, lands and resources and to their related practice of sustainable livelihoods."[9] By defending wilderness, and by articulating our reasons for doing so, we "Transmit to future generations values, traditions, and institutions that support the long-term flourishing of Earth's human and ecological communities."[10]

For those of us who are not indigenous, how do wild lands nourish our spirits?

On my journeys into the Boundary Waters Wilderness of northern Minnesota, my companions and I leave behind the rush of the highway, leave behind the clutter of stores, and launch our canoes into the glossy waters of Fall Lake near the town of Ely. As we paddle across to our first portage, we rock in the wake from motorboats, for gas-powered craft have recently been permitted to cruise the outermost lakes of the wilderness. The manufacturers of outboard motors, ATVs, snowmobiles, and other loud machines are constantly pushing to open every last refuge to invasion by their products, and they are supported by people eager to use those machines, people too lazy or too addicted to power and speed to travel by means of their own muscles.

Crossing Fall Lake, we often hear the boom of radios above the snarl of engines. My companions and I talk loudly to make ourselves heard above the roar. After two portages, however, we drift into Pipestone Bay, which is free of motors, and here for the first time we're likely to see bald eagles, river otters, beavers, and other elusive creatures. In the stillness, we can hear the cries of loons, the splash of leaping fish. We can hear the lap of waves against the bows of the canoes. Here for the first time the buzz of the highway fades, our voices drop, the rhythm of our paddling slows, and we begin to see where we are.

The water is bounded on all sides by rocky shoreline fringed green with pines and hemlocks, white with birches, yellow with poplars. When we land, we find every crack in the granite brilliant with flowers and grass, every square foot of soil carpeted in lichens, liverworts, saplings, and moss. Bears have left black tufts of hair on the bark of trees, and raccoons have left their tracks like hieroglyphics in the damp sand. Not so long ago, this land was barren. It had been clear-cut, trapped out, mined. Then over the decades since being protected as wilderness, the land began to heal—the forest rising again, the animals returning, the streams running clear.

As we travel from lake to lake toward the heart of the Boundary Waters, I can feel my own mind running clear. By the second or third day, the frets and plans I carried from home have fallen away, and I sink into the peacefulness of this place, as into the depths of meditation or prayer. What I sense is not bland comfort, for the wind often blows in our faces as we paddle, cold rain often chills us, and mosquitoes lustily bite. Any one of us could break a leg on a portage, could go crashing over a waterfall, could spill into the water and drown. The peace of this watery wilderness is not the security and ease of a living room, a shopping mall, or any other space controlled by human beings. Wilderness restores our souls precisely because it is *not* controlled by us, because it obeys laws we did not write, because it reminds us of the vast, encompassing order that brought us into being and that moment by moment sustains us.

Even in the Boundary Waters, where every day feels like a sabbath, my companions and I keep track of the calendar, for eventually we must go back home. As we draw near to our launching point, once again we encounter the raucous machines that are gnawing at the edges of the refuge. On the long drive to Indiana, the speed of our car over the pavement seems dizzying. The roadsides seem frantic with billboards and franchises. News from the radio speaks of a crazed and broken world I hardly recognize. Even as I slide back into my ordinary life, which is crowded with too many tasks and too many things, the peace of the wilderness lingers in me like a balm. Even if I never visit the Boundary Waters again, I am nourished by knowing it is there, following its ancient ways, unfettered, free. Every remnant of wilderness, like the sabbath, is a reminder of our origins and our true home.

The sabbath is one-seventh part of our days. Far less than one-seventh part of our land remains in wilderness. If we understand the lessons of restraint and liberation conveyed by the sabbath, then we should leave alone every acre that has not already been stamped by our designs, and we should restore millions of acres that have been abused. We should build no more roads in our national forests. We should cut no more old-growth trees. We should drain no more wetlands. We should neither drill nor prospect in wildlife refuges, allowing those fragile places to be refuges in fact and not only in name. To set land free from serving us is to recognize that Earth is neither our slave nor our property.

Some people object that our economy will falter unless we open up these last scraps of wild land to moneymaking. They warn against the danger of "locking up" resources vital to our prosperity. But couldn't the same be said of the sabbath? Why "lock up" a whole day of the week? Why spend time worshiping, why meditate or pray, when we could be using that time to produce more goods and services? If it is really true that our economy will fail unless we devote every minute and every acre to the pursuit of profit, then our economy is already doomed. For where shall we turn after the calendar and the continent have been exhausted?

Many of the politicians and industry lobbyists who call for the exploitation of our last remaining wild places also claim to be deeply religious. What sort of religion do they follow, if it places no limits on human dominion? What sort of religion do they follow, if it makes the pursuit of profit the central goal of life? If they believe in keeping the sabbath holy, how can they reconcile this commandment with the drive to reduce every acre and every hour to human control? And if they do not believe in keeping the sabbath, how do they pick and choose among the commandments?

To cherish wilderness does not mean that one must despise human works, any more than loving the sabbath means that one must despise the rest of the week. Even if you do not accept the religious premise on which the sabbath is based, as many people do not, then consider the wisdom embodied in the practice of restraint. Through honoring both sabbath and wilderness, we renew our contact with the mystery that precedes and surrounds and upholds our lives. The sabbath and the wilderness remind us of what is true everywhere and at all times, but which in our arrogance we keep forgetting—that we did not make Earth, that we are guests here, that we are answerable to a reality deeper and older and more sacred than our own will.

NOTES

An earlier version of this essay was published under the same title in *Spiritus* 2, no. 2 (fall 2002), published by Johns Hopkins University Press.

1. Earth Charter, Subprinciple 8b.
2. Earth Charter, Subprinciple 15a.
3. Earth Charter, Subprinciple 9c.
4. Earth Charter, Subprinciple 10a.
5. Earth Charter, Subprinciple 1a.
6. Earth Charter, Subprinciple 5e.
7. Earth Charter, Subprinciple 4a.
8. Earth Charter, Subprinciple 5b.
9. Earth Charter, Subprinciple 12b.
10. Earth Charter, Subprinciple 4b.

Who

Robert Michael Pyle

As leaders of nations meet to parley
the state of the Earth, and my country sends
a general, keeping him out of the way back home.
As West Nile virus invades the battered bayous,
and towns beg to be sprayed, palamedes swallowtails
shrivel, and cancers grow commonplace. As water
makes itself scarce out West, Denver desiccates
while Dresden drowns in rains
it could have used in 'forty-five.

As penguins show up in Alaska, and the Antarctic
umbrella frays, Arctic permafrost melts to mush.
As Idaho salmon dwindle to dozens and spuds grow
in chemical mires, Atlantic salmon jump their pens
in the Pacific and California grapes replace oaks.
As pollen of poison maize undoes the monarchs
and Round-up Ready soybeans sack their milkweed,
purple loosestrife bleeds a sterile sward across
the northern marshes, and kudzu consumes
the broadleaf woodlands of the South.

As air and the water run together
in a roily blend, dark night skies and silence
take a powder altogether. As plasterboard palaces
multiply across the meadows, "second home"

for some means a mansion on the hill, while
"fixer-upper" for others is a crate in the barrio.

As Hummers rumble in the towns
where trolleys once ran, motorhomes clog
the open road, and bridges just fall down,
budgets cut bricks and books for bombs.
As half the forests burn and the other half are cut
to keep from burning; as beaches glitter
with hypodermics, and rivers glow with isotopes;
as frogs drop out and reefs bleach whiter than white:
our way of life goes on—
like a suicide bomber in a china shop.

And yet: as soft petals still unfurl,
and bright wings dance on mountain air;
as clear brooks water the high meadows,
and cool breezes bring scents
of balsam and hay; as ash keys
and maple samaras and hazelnuts yet drop
on moist forest floors *in spite of it all*,
the Earth is not yet lost . . .

and, as I consider these verbs from its *Charter*:

serve affirm accept build ensure promote
secure protect adopt establish safeguard
control prevent manage advance convert
reduce reuse recycle rely relieve require
resolve restore respect recognize support
guarantee empower enable strengthen
uphold fulfill create enhance eliminate
integrate institute implement demilitarize
care honor act

I wonder:
Who will care? Who will honor? Who will act?
Who?

Broad Water, Distant Land

Stuart Ching

> "You're lucky," he says. "You got the Hawaiian look. You can pass."
>
> my father, to me, as far back as I can remember . . .

> Affirm the right of indigenous peoples to their spirituality, knowledge, lands and resources and to their related practice of sustainable livelihoods.
>
> Earth Charter, Principle 12b

When I was a boy, at our yearly family parties at *Popo's* (Grandmother's) house in Kapahulu, amid the kitchen smells of fried noodles, crispy *gaugee*, and roasted chicken, one Chinese aunt would gaze admiringly at me and say, "Stuart look like Hawaiian boy. Stuart no look like Chinese boy!"

"Ho shoo!" *Popo* would brag, "All the senior citizens at Paki Park ask me, 'Your grandson part-Hawaiian? Your son marry Hawaiian?' Yah, Stuart look like Hawaiian boy."

Throughout my childhood, I passed as Hawaiian. Many years later as an adult, I began differentiating passing as Hawaiian and truly advocating Hawaiian indigenous rights. Like the protagonist in my story "Broad Water, Distant Land," motivated by a deep respect for the native people of Hawai'i, I eschewed the former and embraced the latter.

Advocating native rights in Hawai'i, however, is far from simple. Native Hawaiian activist and scholar Haunani-Kay Trask has explained U.S. colonization of Hawai'i: through the introduction of fatal diseases against which the native population in ancient times had no natural immunization; through the usurpation of the Hawaiian land base; through the capitalist exploitation of Hawai'i's goods, indigenous people, and native culture; through education; through language; and through religion. Trask further notes that, since 1954, descendents of plantation immigrants who were marginalized and, themselves, colonized during Hawai'i's plantation era have gained economic and political power in the state. In wielding their newly acquired economic and political power, these descendents have participated in the colonization of Hawai'i's indigenous people.[1] Moreover, as cultural studies scholar Walter Mignolo reminds us, colonialism is at once everywhere: traversing oceans and penetrating the body.[2] Decolonizing the popular imagination and consciousness, then, is no easy task. It involves work on all fronts: revitalization of culture and cultural sites; restoration of a Hawaiian land base; reallocation of natural resources and capital; reeducation of native and nonnative people on Hawai'i's indigenous cultural and spiritual values; and, from nonnative peoples, advocacy for native causes.

Principle 12 of the Earth Charter advocates all of these actions. It states:

> Uphold the right of all, without discrimination, to a natural and social environment supportive of human dignity, bodily health, and spiritual well-being, with special attention to the rights of indigenous peoples and minorities.
>
> a. Eliminate discrimination in all its forms, such as that based on race, color, sex, sexual orientation, religion, language, and national, ethnic or social origin.
>
> b. Affirm the right of indigenous peoples to their spirituality, knowledge, lands and resources and to their related practice of sustainable livelihoods.
>
> c. Honor and support the young people of our communities, enabling them to fulfill their essential role in creating sustainable societies.
>
> d. Protect and restore outstanding places of cultural and spiritual significance.

Yet, despite the enormous good will driving the document, the Earth Charter is at once inspiring and fraught, unifying and conflicted. Principle 12 exemplifies this inherent tension and complexity. It gains its ethical power by supporting the disenfranchised; it simultaneously detracts from this power by conflating minorities and indigenous peoples. It gains inspirational strength by championing democratic ideals such as those in the U.S. Constitution; it simultaneously fails to recognize that assumed equality founded on the discourses of race and constitutionality—rather than on genealogy and native rights that predate imperialist conquest—has historically threatened and, in some cases, derailed the sovereignty and reclamation movements of indigenous peoples. Principle 12 also inspiringly envisions a global citizen; it simultaneously fails to recognize that global citizenship in the present era is, at best, an ideal, at worst, a myth. As postcolonial scholar Tomo Hattori reminds us, in our conflicted contemporary times, the ideal of global citizenship gives way to other "institutions" of enormous power and "reach," among these, "capital, religion, terrorism."[3]

Noting these contradictions in the Earth Charter is not cynicism; rather, calling attention to these tensions affirms the Earth Charter's purpose. I view the Earth Charter as an exhortation, a call for dialogue and action, and a cry for Earth. It begins: "We stand at a critical moment in Earth's history, a time when humanity must choose its future."[4] To choose wisely and ethically, we must conceptualize and articulate our options in their full complexity and greatest clarity. Far from a conclusion, then, the Earth Charter opens up a space—outside the rigid borders of nations, institutionalized faiths, and globalized economic networks—for dialogue, inquiry, and deliberation that can inform and sustain the difficult work to be done.

In the space of my own imagination, "Broad Water, Distant Land" is my attempt within a local site to grapple with some of the complex global ideals and issues that the Earth Charter introduces, to enliven its principles against the legacy and consequences of colonialism in Hawai'i, and to further a dialogue that may contribute to a sustainable Hawai'i and world.

Dad and I searched the horizon for bumps, the smallest folds in Earth's curve. My father, a long-time surfer, had taught me the patterns of big late-summer waves. They start at distant epicenters, a tremor in Japan, a hurricane in Tahiti. If not for continents and islands, he explained, waves are nomadic. They travel forever.

"Like Mr. Alama's ghost," I said. "Kenny said Mr. Alama get plenty unfinished business."

"You reading too much *obake* stories, Howard-boy. No such thing as ghosts. Sometimes when people sad and confused, they try for bring back the dead. Kenny should let Mr. Alama rest. Things are as they are."

In the early morning light, two lovers strolled barefoot along Waikīkī Beach. A jogger crossed the beach walk connecting the Moana and Outrigger Hotels. Dad and I walked toward the shoreline, scattering a flock of pigeons. Then we slipped quietly like interlopers into the sea.

The Alama family had lived in a rental house near Manono's Grocers and J. H. C. Auto Body Repair. Mr. Alfred Alama had been the eldest in the house occupied by three generations of Alamas. His granddaughter Wanda and his grandson, Kenny, attended my school, Jarrett Intermediate. Shortly after Mr. Alama died, Kenny told me that one evening the youngest grandchild, Noelani, saw Mr. Alama sleeping in his La-Z-Boy chair. Mr. Alama's widow, Puanani, sniffed the chair's cracked vinyl. "Alfred stay," she said. "I smell him." The next morning, Kenny's mom found Puanani Alama asleep in the living room.

"Ma, don't tell me you slept in this chair all night!"

"He talk to me," Puanani had said. "Alfred tell me things, all kind things."

Whatever Mr. Alama's ghost had whispered, Dad seemed right. *Things are as they are.* Denied lease renegotiation and evicted along with the neighboring businesses, the Alamas moved to Pālolo Housing, the city project crowding the northeast side of Pālolo Valley. Bulldozers leveled the entire block. Two weeks later, Pacific Masonry poured the concrete foundation for the new condominium development. Dad, the owner of Tanabe Roofing, Framing, and Interiors, surveyed the site. The next Saturday he began construction.

I was only thirteen, too young for employment, but Dad let me earn extra money on weekends. So on Saturday, wearing a yellow hard hat and boots with steel toes, I climbed up and down the scaffolds, running tools and hardware to the carpenters. At noon, when the men opened their lunch boxes and guzzled water from their coolers, I opened my *bento* box and gobbled down my rice balls and *teriyaki* chicken. After lunch, Dad handed me the garden hose, and I walked the grounds, spraying the soil to prevent dust.

That evening, I called Kenny, and the next morning, we rode our bicycles to Waikīkī. Dad had made two surfboard bicycle racks—each an eighteen-inch-long steel clip padded with foam—and had mounted them on the back tires of our bicycles. For most kids, the five miles from Pālolo to Waikīkī was impossible by bicycle—carrying a surfboard under one arm and steering with the other was hazardous on the narrow, hilly, and heavily trafficked streets of Kaimukī and upper Kapahulu. But with our racks, we weaved skillfully through traffic, both hands gripping the handlebars, our surfboards catching air behind us like sails.

At Waikīkī, we parked our bicycles at the surfboard and canoe rental stand run by the local beach boys. Charlie Kamana, a muscular silver-haired old-timer, approached. "Sorry to hear about Grandpa Alama," he said to Kenny. "Me and Alfred go way back, from Pearl Harbor shipyard, over thirty years before I retire. Tell your grandma any time she need help for mow the lawn or do repairs around the house, whatever, Charlie said for call him. Me and the other beach boys can help out."

"Thanks, Mr. Kamana," said Kenny. "But we got evicted. We stay at Pālolo Housing."

"Huh?" said Charlie. "Since when?"

"Couple weeks," said Kenny. "Going have townhouses."

"One shame," said Charlie, shaking his head. "One damn shame."

I looked down and poked the sand with my toes.

Kenny and I walked to the water, waxed our surfboards, and paddled past the tourists floating on rubber rafts. Soon we lost ourselves in the late-morning surf—lines and lines of big summer waves. On his last ride, Kenny stood atop a mountain of water, pressing his arms into the sky. The offshore winds rained ocean spray on him. He slid downward. The wave bent and curled up and over him, tucking him inside a glimmering skin of water. In the channel, I crooned my neck and shouted. Nearby, the grey-haired and wrinkled old-timers paddling long boards howled, "Ahhooohhh!"

"Ahhooohhh!" Kenny yelled back.

Like Hawaiian monk seals, old and young surfers howled, "Ahhooohhh! Ahhoooohhh!"

On the way home, Kenny and I stopped at Rainbow Drive-in. We ordered plate lunches and found a table in the crowded open-air dining area. "Hold your breath," I said. "The Orchid Man coming." The Orchid Man wore a soiled blue *aloha* shirt and khaki trousers with a hole over the left knee. He pushed a shopping cart piled with blankets and an old jacket. On the side of his cart dangled plastic bags filled with flowers. He placed a plumeria next to Kenny's plate.

"Thanks, brah," said Kenny. The Orchid Man nodded and pushed his cart to an empty table. We dug into our plate lunches, and when I finally paused to drink some fruit punch, I spied the Orchid Man eyeing us.

"Watch out, brah," I said to Kenny. "I think he hungry."

"You *pau,* Howard?" said Kenny. "Finish already?"

"Almost," I said. Kenny neatly pushed half of his chili, rice, and macaroni salad to one side of his plate. Then he scooped my barbecue meat on the other half. "What you doing?" I said. He walked to the Orchid Man.

"Here, brah," Kenny said. The Orchid Man placed the plate atop his cart, then reached into his plastic bag and handed Kenny a purple orchid.

"This flower more better," the Orchid Man said. "Go take home for your mother."

"You nuts," I said to Kenny when he returned to the table. "The Orchid Man *hauna.* He stink. He one hippie! You know where he got that orchid? From behind the Thai restaurant. One time I seen him digging inside the dumpster." But Kenny was watching the Orchid Man push his cart into the parking lot, and onto the sidewalk, and across the street toward the Ala Wai Canal.

When we reached Pālolo Valley, Kenny invited me to his apartment. I recalled Mom's caution, *Stay away from the Projects. Only hobos and vagrants live there.* But Kenny was already pulling ahead, leading me toward Pālolo Housing. Kenny lived on the ground floor. We parked our bicycles on the lanai and stepped into the cramped unit.

"Who's that?" called someone.

"Me," said Kenny. "Me and Howard." I peeked out from the kitchen into the living room. Mrs. Alama was sitting with her eyes closed in the La-Z-Boy rocker-recliner. Before her, Wanda was kneeling and dipping a sponge into a tin basin. She gently dabbed Mrs. Alama's arms and palms, her fingers. Then she lifted Mrs. Alama's faded *mu'umu'u* and sponged her thighs and knees and calves. She held each of Mrs. Alama's feet and sponged underneath and then between the toes. "Ohhh, good, good," Mrs. Alama said. Wanda placed the sponge in the basin and propped two pillows behind Mrs. Alama. She sprinkled baby powder on Mrs. Alama's feet, massaged the powder between her toes, and then rocked the La-Z-Boy gently.

Kenny opened the cabinet beneath the sink and pulled out an empty mayonnaise jar. He filled the jar with water and placed the orchid inside. Then he walked into the living room and set the jar on the folding table. "Here, Grandma," he said, kissing Mrs. Alama's cheek. "I got this for you."

Kenny grabbed his skateboard and we stepped outside. We walked across the parking lot to the driveway, which sloped some thirty yards and opened on Pālolo Avenue. Kenny skated first, zigzagging and looping as though surfing a gigantic wave. I rode next. A yellow Volkswagen van sped into the driveway and screeched in front of me. The board shot from under my feet and struck the van's bumper. I landed on my backside. A large Hawaiian boy stepped out of the van. This was Mason Kamakau, Kaimukī High School's all-state defensive tackle. He grabbed my armpits and hoisted me to my feet. He turned to Kenny. "Driveways for cars, Kenny-boy. You like skate, go to the drainage ditch." He pointed down the hill toward the intermediate school and Pālolo District Park. Behind the park ran a storm drain bordered by a chain link fence.

"Guys smoke dope over there," said Kenny. "They ask us for money. If we no give, they tell us, 'Search-take.' Then they hijack us."

"Who?" said Mason. "Who went hijack you guys?"

"Kirk Omatsu, Dennis Sasaki, and some other high school surfer guys."

Kenny and I described how Kirk and Dennis had robbed us in the ditch. Shaking the chain link fence above us, Kirk had yelled, "Eh! This one toll ditch! Ten dollar fee."

"This city and county property," Kenny said.

"You calling me one liar?" said Kirk. He climbed over the fence and stumbled down the drainage-ditch wall. Dennis followed, sliding down the concrete embankment on his backside. I heard his shorts tearing.

"Burn your ass!" said Kenny.

"Ha-ha-ha!" I said, sticking my middle finger at Dennis.

Kenny and I ran. Someone wrestled me from behind. I heard Kenny smack the concrete beside me. "Where your money?" Dennis said, pinning me to the ground. His big hands and fingers dug into my pockets.

"No more nothing!" I said. He stood and pulled off my shoes. "See," I said. "I told you. I no more!" He yanked off my socks. A twenty-dollar bill fell to the ground.

"Fricken liar," said Dennis.

Kirk scrambled for the money.

"I going tell my father!" Kenny said, struggling to stand. "I going call the cops!"

"Shit," said Kirk. He walked back to Kenny and squeezed Kenny's mouth. "You tell on us, I going bust your face!" Kirk pushed Kenny to the ground and smashed his face into the asphalt.

Dennis jammed a sock into my mouth. "Eat that," he said. Then he and Kirk ran down the storm drain toward Waiʻalae Avenue, laughing. Kenny stood, dusting the gravel from his knees and elbows. His left eye was swollen. A piece of glass was stuck in his cheek. I pulled the glass out and took off my shirt.

"Here, brah," I said. He took the shirt and pressed it against his cheek.

"Fricken Japs," Kenny had said. "One day I going get them. One day . . ."

Now Mason shook his head. "Next time you see Omatsu and Sasaki, tell those two Japs I looking for them. Tell them I going kick their ass."

I'd seen my share of ass-kicking, growing up a local Japanese kid in Hawai'i, especially on every December 7, which for local Japanese kids had two names: Bomb Pearl Harbor Day and Slap-a-Jap Day. Every December 7, at least a third of the Japanese kids feigned illness. Mom, a teacher at Kaimukī High School, would gripe at dinner. "Today in home room I had five menstrual cramps, six diarrheas, three twenty-four-hour flus, three toothaches, and five driver's tests." Once I asked Mom to call Jarrett Intermediate's attendance office for me, but she said, "Howard-boy, don't hide your Japanese heritage. You're Japanese, but you're local Japanese. Japanese American. Your Uncle Takami fought for the United States in World War II. Your Uncle Bert fought in Vietnam, earned the Purple Heart. That scar on his leg, that's from a bullet wound. Your ancestors, they sailed all the way from Okinawa, from the fishing village of Yonabaru, way back. They're part of the island's plantation history—they helped lead the great strike in 1920 that made work better for everybody. Your family paid with blood for this island, in fact, for this country. Your ancestors brought their dreams across the ocean and planted them here. You grew from that seed. You understand? This is our home as much as anybody's."

And so I, along with other local Japanese kids, braved December 7. In commemoration of Bomb Pearl Harbor Day the tough kids in school of non-Japanese ancestry leaned over the second story railing of C-building and bombed the Japanese kids with opened milk cartons. In honor of "Slap-a-Jap-Day," the tough kids waited in the restrooms and pummeled you. But in some ways, I was luckier than the fair-skinned, thin, and hairless Japanese boys. I was stocky and hairy like most Okinawans of the southern farming and fishing villages of the Japanese empire. The Japanese considered Okinawans yokels, country bumpkins. We had thick and stumpy appendages, *daikon*, or radish legs. We were dark, chocolate brown—almost black in my case. My Okinawan features, bushy eyebrows, large eyes, and a Roman nose, suggested that I might be a mixed-blood, maybe *hapa:* part Hawaiian, part Filipino, or part Puerto Rican. Especially when I hung out with Kenny, I could pass. I could dodge the perils of "Bomb Pearl Harbor Day."

After Dad's carpenters completed the framing, his roofers arrived. They cut plywood sheets and nailed them to the rafters. When they completed the plywood layer, I joined them on the roof and helped spread the tarp. Over the tarp, the roofers mopped tar, then nailed down the composite shingles. Bang! Bang! Bang! Their hammers pounded the wood like rocks plummeting from the sky. Amid the clamor, I stood at the roof's highest point and gazed over Pālolo Valley. I saw, across the valley, the roof of my house tucked amid several palms. Toward the ocean, I saw the telephone and electrical lines marking the roads and, beyond, the crater of Diamond Head. Toward the mountains, I saw the Pālolo Housing Project. Then I saw Kenny riding his bicycle down the street.

"Kenny!" I shouted, waving. Kenny stopped by Dad's work truck. He looked at me. "Kenny!" I called again. Kenny circled back up the street, turned, and then sped down the hill toward a piece of plywood propped against stacked lumber. He bolted off the make-shift ramp. He soared in the air like a miniature Evil Knievel. "Kenny!" I called. He landed and stuck his middle finger in the air. He sped down Pālolo Avenue, not looking back.

On Monday, Kenny ignored me in school. Mrs. Soares, our social studies teacher, announced the class's fall thematic unit, Hawai'i's Mixed Plate Lunch. She divided the class into research teams. Each team would research a different part of Hawai'i's population: Filipino, Korean, Japanese, Chinese, Portuguese, Hawaiian. Each team was a different part of the mixed plate: team one was the Filipino pickled pork, or *adobo*; team two was the Japanese fried chicken, or *katsu*; team three was the Korean spicy fermented cabbage, or *kim chee*; team four was the Chinese dumpling, or *gaugee*; team five was the Hawaiian taro, or *poi*. Mrs. Soares said Hawai'i was better than the mainland melting pot and salad bowl. Hawai'i was the delicious plate lunch! So many rich flavors! Then she took us to the library, where Mrs. Shimizu, the librarian, distributed our research packets. My team—Esther Horibata, Jasmine Takeuchi, Kenny, and I—sat around our assigned rectangular table. Esther, the eighth-grade student government president and our self-appointed team leader, announced that we were in charge of Hawaiian Culture.

"You and Kenny do this part," she said, handing me a folder labeled "Contemporary Hawaiians in the News." Among the articles were news clippings on Kimo Mitchell, George Helm, and Eddie Aikau. All three had been lost at sea. Helm and Mitchell disappeared mysteriously into high surf off the coast of Kaho'olawe while protesting the U.S. military's bombing of the island in 1977. Aikau was a famous Hawaiian lifeguard renowned for surfing the biggest waves at Waimea Bay. In 1978 he joined the Hōkūle'a Canoe, the small vessel that sailed the ancient Hawaiian migration route between Tahiti and Hawai'i. On its second historical voyage, the canoe capsized in stormy open seas between O'ahu and Moloka'i. Seeking help, Aikau mounted his surfboard and, as his crew clinging to the capsized canoe prayed for him, he disappeared into the broad, mountainous swells, paddling for land. He had never been seen again.

"Try read this," I told Kenny. "Unreal, these guys."

He pushed the articles away and looked down. He continued sketching a wave on his folder. "How come you never tell me your father was the one who went evict us?" he said.

"Wasn't him," I said.

"Who the hell went bulldoze our house?" said Kenny. "That wasn't you on the roof? Waving like one fricken jackass!"

"My father only the contractor," I said. "The owner and developer . . . they live in California. I just go on weekends. Not my fault."

"Shit," Kenny said.

Mrs. Shimizu approached us. "Boys, I worked hard to prepare this material. You should be reading, not talking." I returned to my article. Kenny slouched in his chair, furrowed his brows, and poked his tablet with his pencil. Mrs. Shimizu placed an article in front of Kenny. She tapped it with her finger. "How are you going to report intelligently about your topic if you don't read? Do you know why Kaho'olawe was in the news?"

Kenny pushed the paper away. “Kahoʻolawe not one *topic*,” he said to Mrs. Shimizu. “Kahoʻolawe one sacred place. The military went bomb our land. First the Japs bomb Pearl Harbor. Then the *haoles* bomb Kahoʻolawe. No try tell me Kahoʻolawe one research topic. My grandpa went teach me all I need for know. Bombing Kahoʻolawe is one *desecration*.” Mrs. Shimizu’s face flushed.

“Kenny!” said Mrs. Soares, approaching. “Mrs. Shimizu is trying to help you.”

“I no need help!” he said, motioning at me. “My family got evicted by this jackass’s father! You see anybody helping us?”

“Cool it, brah,” I said.

“Shut up, Howard, before I blast you!” said Kenny. Mrs. Soares stepped between us.

“Everybody just wants to help,” she said to Kenny. “Mrs. Shimizu, your friends, they care for you.”

“What kind friend would kick me out of my house?” he said. Then he looked at me. “Huh, Howard, what kind friend is that?” Mrs. Soares ordered me to an open table across the library. Esther and Jasmine followed. The eighth-grade counselor, Mr. Ebert, took Kenny to the office. I tried to read the articles, but my thoughts drifted back to Kenny. Eventually, I folded my arms and rested my head on the table, listening to the valley wind whirring through the library’s open louvers. Finally, the bell rang.

After the subcontractors completed the plumbing and electrical wiring, Dad’s crew began installing the counter cabinets and dry wall. Even before he finished the interior, prospective buyers began visiting the on-site sales office. One day, Mrs. Alama and her family arrived. All six of them, the elder Mrs. Alama, Kenny’s father and mother, Wanda, little Noelani, and Kenny, entered the air-conditioned portable office trailer. I walked to a far corner of the lot and started raking stray candy wrappers and paper cups. The trailer door opened, and the Alamas exited with the sales representative, a petite Japanese woman named Alice. Kenny’s father held Mrs. Alama’s left arm as she hobbled with her cane down the trailer steps. Then Alice took the Alamas into one of the model units. They exited and stood at the entry, talking. Kenny picked up a wooden stick and drummed on one of the columns. Alice glared at him. "Boy, put the stick down," his father said. Kenny flung the stick and then walked toward the trailer, kicking rocks and aluminum cans along the way. He sat on the trailer steps.

Alice opened her portfolio, pointing to various parts of the lot. "Let's tour the grounds." She walked on the pathway, pausing now and then for Mrs. Alama, and stopped where the concrete ended some ten yards away from me. "A courtyard will be here," said Alice, "and, over there, a walkway to a small play area for children, swing set, climbing apparatus. Back there we'll have a pavilion, and at the edge of the property, there's a gorgeous view of Pālolo Valley. Let's go look."

"I seen enough already," said Mrs. Alama. "I used to live here. This was my backyard. Had one mango tree. Alfred and me used to sit in the shade, eat boiled peanuts, listen to the mynah birds. Had one stream running through the yard, and the toads and frogs hide in the mandu grass. The sound of water remind us of the ocean. Alfred love the water, his second home. He love to fish. I thought Alfred and me . . . I thought. . . ." She shook her head and looked back toward the townhouses. "You see what they doing, Alfred? Pretty soon I be with you."

"Ma, no talk like that," said Kenny's father.

Mrs. Alama began hobbling back toward the parking lot. Dad came out of one of the units, a set of blueprints rolled in one hand. "And you!" Mrs. Alama said, moving toward Dad, poking her cane at him. "The kind prices you guys charge. How we can afford?" She closed in on Dad, her face just inches from his. "Shame on you," she said. "Shame on you!"

"Come, Mom," said Kenny's dad, pulling Mrs. Alama's arm. "Let's go."

"Grab your sister's hand," Kenny's mom said to Wanda, pushing her toward Noelani. "Follow your grandma." Hobbling on her cane, Mrs. Alama led her family to the car. Dad looked down and shook his head.

That was the last time I saw Mrs. Alama, but years later, on the evening news coverage of Hawaiian activists protesting the H-3 Freeway's construction over sacred Hawaiian burial grounds, I would see a woman say these exact words. The camera zoomed in on a stooped and grayed Hawaiian woman bearing down on a police barricade. She pressed into a Hawaiian officer, his face visible even through his riot gear. "Shame on you!" the woman said. "Shame on you for desecrating your ancestors' sacred land!"

The day after the Alamas visited the property, landscape engineers set up their surveying instruments. Soon, masons completed the concrete walkways, walls, sitting areas, and water features—a fountain and a small koi pond. Garden landscapers planted assorted ground cover and flowers—birds of paradise, roses, mock orange hedges. Road workers tarred and painted the parking lot.

In school, Mrs. Soares announced Mrs. Alama's death, and she asked each of us to sign a condolence card.

"How Mrs. Alama died?" I said after class.

"I don't know," said Mrs. Soares. "Mr. Ebert said she was ill. Or sometimes old people die of a broken heart. I heard her husband passed away recently."

I nodded. "You think Kenny would be mad if I go to the funeral?"

"You need to do what you feel," said Mrs. Soares.

At Waikīkī, my parents and I stood high up on the beach, near the snack shop by the canoe rentals and the Moana Hotel. Along with some of the beach boys and a few cousins and uncles, Kenny paddled out to sea, carrying Mrs. Alama's urn. On shore, the mourners gathered near the water in a half-circle opening on the sea. I started toward them.

"Come on," I said, motioning to my parents.

"Go, Howard-Boy," Dad said. "We wait here. Go pay respects." I walked to the shoreline and stood several feet outside the circle. I cupped my hand over my eyes and squinted against the sun reflecting off the ocean. Kenny paddled into the surf and released Mrs. Alama's ashes. Then the procession of surfers began paddling toward shore. When the surfers returned, they laid their boards on the sand and waded into the shallows, joining hands with the others and closing the circle into one body connecting land and sea. An elder—perhaps a *kupuna*, a respected bearer of knowledge—began chanting in Hawaiian. His high-pitched, nasal falsetto displaced the laughter of tourists, eclipsed the sound of trolleys trafficking nearby Kalākaua Avenue. I nudged my way into the circle. Across from me stood Kenny, his thin and wiry frame wet and glistening as though birthed from the sea. He was weeping.

I remember something Dad said during the ride home, "Too bad about Mrs. Alama. All that bitterness no good. That's what took her to the grave. The only way the Hawaiians going make it nowadays is to forgive and forget. Gotta move on." And as the Buick glided down Kapahulu Avenue, past storefronts and low-rise apartment buildings, then up into the hills of Kaimukī toward Pālolo Valley, I thought about how I'd stood on the shore, remembering Mrs. Alama, and how I couldn't forget—the memory of her voice, the tide washing over my bare feet, Kenny nodding at me. I wondered what would happen to Mrs. Alama's spirit, her ashes already scattering on the seafloor, mingling with the coral, drifting with the tide.

NOTES

1. Haunani-Kay Trask. "Hawaiians, American Colonization, and the Quest for Independence." *Social Process in Hawaii: A Reader.* Ed. Peter Manicas. New York: McGraw-Hill, 1993, 1–19.

2. Walter Mignolo. *Local Histories/Global Designs: Coloniality, Subaltern Knowledges, and Border Thinking.* Princeton: Princeton University Press, 2000, ix.

3. Tomo Hattori and Stuart H. D. Ching. "Re-Examining the Between-Worlds Trope in Cross-Cultural Composition Studies." Paper presented for the panel "Representations: Doing Asian American Rhetoric" at the Rhetoric Society of America 13th Biennial Conference, Seattle, May 23–26, 2008.

4. Earth Charter, Preamble, paragraph one.

Possibility Begins Here

Lauret Savoy

Once I was a horse, an Appaloosa wild and full of speed. I would run fast—up and down sidewalks, around the school playground and our yard—just to feel wind rush with me and, sometimes, to run away from what I feared. In the late 1960s the world seemed to have moved beyond sense: race riots near our home, the Vietnam "war" and its casualties, killings of "good" men, and in my own family palpable silence and bitterness.

At eight years of age I came to know and fear hatred-filled words spat on me because of my brown skin. One sharp memory among many: a gray fall morning on the school playground; a classmate's sing-song *never saw nothin' as ugly as a nigger, never saw nothin' as crummy as a nigger*; his eyes on me. Then running home to my closet floor where everything but *that* word lost its color in darkness. I remember holding knees tightly to my chest, rocking through tears, wondering *What does my skin say? What does my skin say?*

Forced to confront imposed "racial" difference long before understanding it, I, like many children, questioned my identity and authenticity in the world. I avoided mirrors. Emotional nourishment and refuge came from being outdoors in a nature that never judged me, whether in city parks of Los Angeles or Washington, D.C., or in wilder mountains and deserts. Voice only began to come much later, question by question, in teenage encounters with writings that urged me to look beneath appearances and take nothing for granted. The authors—like Rachel Carson or Viktor Frankl or Franz Fanon—seemed themselves to be seeking.

I first read Aldo Leopold's *A Sand County Almanac* for a ninth-grade assignment. His enlargement of "the boundaries of the community to include soil, water, plants, animals, or collectively: the land" and his call for an extension of ethics to land relations seemed to articulate senses of responsibility and reciprocity not embraced by the U. S. of A., but embedded in indigenous peoples' traditions of experience—that land has immediate presence, that it is intimate and fully inhabited.[1] To a fourteen-year-old the troubling possibility of Leopold's "land ethic" forced new questions. *If "obligations have no meaning without conscience," then what part of this nation has lacked conscience broad enough for Americans, as individuals and a whole, to realize the necessary internal change of mind and heart, to embrace this "evolutionary possibility" and "ecological necessity"?*[2] The history taught to me in school either praised or simply presented the material fruits of Euro-America's manifest destiny as inevitable. *Yet how was I or those who looked like me a part of this history? What did it mean to be African American and mixedblood in this America?* Only estrangement and uncertainty felt within reach, as if Leopold's "we" excluded me and others with ancestral roots in Africa, Asia, or Native America.

Although more than a score years have passed, the questions of a fourteen-year-old persist and feed larger ones. *What will it take for us, as citizens of a nation and of the world, to understand how we exist in relation to each other and the land in time and space? What would it then take for us to live that interdependence responsibly? What is possible?*

The Earth Charter is a "declaration of fundamental principles for building a just, sustainable, and peaceful global society for the 21st century."[3] The principles offer frames of possibility for international and cross-cultural partnerships based on shared responsibility and interdependence. Respect and care for the community of life. Ecological integrity. Social and economic justice. Democracy, nonviolence, and peace.

The challenge we all face is to imagine existence broadly, as children might, and to seek common ground where edges have separated us. Natural history and human history, natural and cultural diversity, social and ecological conscience—none is easily separable from the other. Yet ecological interdependence between human beings and the land, broadly defined, is framed by a history that informs our senses of place on Earth and our connections with each other.

> History . . . is not merely something to be read. And it does not refer merely, or even principally, to the past. On the contrary, the great force of history comes from the fact that we carry it within us, are unconsciously controlled by it in many ways, and history is literally present in all that we do. . . . And it is with great pain and terror that one begins to realize this. In great pain and terror one begins to assess the history which has placed one where one is and formed one's point of view. In great pain and terror because, therefore, one enters into battle with that historical creation, Oneself.[4]

Deeply rooted social and economic values, norms, and institutions in this country continue to marginalize the natural world in fragmenting ecosystems, threatening biological diversity, and changing the nature of our atmosphere through the burning of fossil fuels. Their roots also fed systems that promoted the enslavement of African peoples, and the dispossession and forced removal of aboriginal peoples from homeland to reservation more than a century ago. Yet who has honestly faced how these things might be linked today to what marginalizes the lives of children born in ghettos or on reservations in a country whose societal structures continue to feed a material and spiritual poverty, and cultural erosion and despair?

With origins in all parts of the world, every one of us in this nation inherits and shares the legacies of its development. Euro-America's manifest destiny across a continental "wilderness" owed much to colonizing processes, to the enslavement, exile, and exclusion of peoples of color in a deeply racialized American society. The compromising of nature, and the compromising of human beings by racialism and inequities in political and economic power, contribute to *our* multicultural past and present. Witness poor communities of color that continue to suffer disproportionate levels of environmental pollution and toxicity. Witness the curtailing of civil rights and cutting back of even basic assistance to the poor and disenfranchised.

As a descendant of slaves and freemen, native inhabitants, and colonizers from Europe, I struggle to understand what it means for me—or anyone—to be an American and a human being. Frames of bondage, segregation, forced removal, and an ancient connection to homeland shaped how my ancestors experienced the world and who they knew themselves to be in that world. The legacies of those frames shape us still, their presence malignant to the degree they have been ignored, forgotten, or silenced and then repeated in institutions, and in people's attitudes and lives.

There may be many things about ourselves that my countrymen and -women do not wish to know, but ignorance of human diversity and human contradiction only nourishes social injustice and ecological denial. Ideals of freedom, democracy, and independence ring hollow—and false—if they remain accessible to a privileged few, the rest of us meant to be kept invisible, silent.

In December 1948 the recently formed United Nations General Assembly voted to accept the Universal Declaration of Human Rights. One hope was that this document would, in Eleanor Roosevelt's words, "establish standards for human rights and freedom the world over." The language in the preamble is clear:

> Whereas recognition of the inherent dignity and of the equal and inalienable rights of all members of the human family is the foundation of freedom, justice and peace in the world,
>
> Whereas disregard and contempt for human rights have resulted in barbarous acts which have outraged the conscience of mankind, and the advent of a world in which human beings shall enjoy freedom of speech and belief and freedom from fear and want has been proclaimed as the highest aspiration of the common people, . . .[5]

Yet the United States objected to ratification, as the Assistant Secretary of State for Public Affairs Edward Barrett wrote around 1950: "Neither the Executive Branch nor the Congress would desire that our Government should ratify a convention which contains obligations that our Government and our people are unwilling or unable to honor."[6]

What obligations might our government and our people be unwilling or unable to honor, beyond ideals, today?

The word *conscience* comes from the Latin *conscientia*, a joint knowledge or feeling, from *conscire* (*com-*, together with; and *scire*, to know). Obligations have no meaning without conscience, without an acceptance of ethical responsibility.

It is here that the Earth Charter has a role to play. Respect and care for the community of life. Ecological integrity. Social and economic justice. Democracy, nonviolence, and peace. The four parts of the Earth Charter, taken together, contribute to a joint knowledge, and call for open and inclusive exchange, participation, cooperation, solidarity, and mutual understanding of all peoples of the world.

But what is possible?

We fail ourselves and our children to live with less than the largest possible sense of community, and we fool ourselves to live as if the past is no longer part of us. Mustn't citizens of this or any nation go beyond myth, face hypocrisy and contradiction, terror as well as beauty, to understand the complex dynamics that have shaped the land and ourselves as people? Only then, I believe, can a larger sense of who we are and where we are as interconnected ecological, cultural, and historical beings begin to develop. If, as Aldo Leopold wrote, the health of the land is its capacity for self-renewal, then perhaps the health of the human family may in part be an intergenerational capacity for locating ourselves within many inheritances as citizens of the land, of nations, and of Earth, and thus within ever-widening communities.

These are communities that respect Earth and life in all its diversity. Communities that build democratic societies that are just, participatory, sustainable, and peaceful. Communities that promote a culture of tolerance, nonviolence, and peace. That affirm gender equality and equity. That uphold the rights of all, without discrimination, to a natural and social environment supportive of human dignity. That eradicate the roots of poverty. That strengthen democratic institutions at all levels, and provide transparency and accountability in governance, inclusive participation in decision making, and access to justice. These principles from the Earth Charter can become a collective vision.

Memories cut, and years past my childhood I still tend to avoid mirrors. But to face myself I try to look beyond the reflection to accreted layers of heritage, of questions, of living. Silence, invisibility, and escape never were options—and are not now. Beneath the layers, wonder, wind, and scent of wild horse still exist. *Possibility begins here for me.*

Where does possibility begin for you?

NOTES

1. Aldo Leopold. "The Land Ethic." A *Sand County Almanac*. Oxford: Oxford University Press, 1949, 204.

2. Ibid., 209, 203.

3. The Earth Charter Initiative, <http://www.earthcharter.org/>.

4. James Baldwin. "White Man's Guilt" (1965). *The Price of the Ticket: Collected Nonfiction 1948–1985*. New York: St. Martin's Press, 1985, 410.

5. Universal Declaration of Human Rights, Preamble, <http://www.un.org/Overview/rights.html>.

6. Quoted in J. Saunders Redding. *On Being Negro in America*. New York: Bantam, 1951, 96, 99.

Hope for Democracy

Janisse Ray

The morning after the 2004 presidential election my husband thinks that I'm sleeping and silently gets out of bed. It's 5:00 A.M. I've lain awake an hour, wondering who will be our president come January. I remember a time when our country went to bed on Election Night knowing the outcome, but since the election of 2000, nothing is certain. I find Raven downstairs, listening to the radio in the Vermont dark.

"Still undecided," he says grimly.

"How can that be?"

"Florida went to Bush, so he's in the lead. There are two points between him and Kerry."

"Are all the results in?"

"Not Ohio. It's held up by provisional ballots. The Democrats want all of them counted."

"So this time it's Ohio instead of Florida," I say.

"Perhaps."

"We've lost."

"There's still a chance. Ohio could go to Kerry." Raven and I voted for Kerry in our home state of Georgia, having only recently moved to Vermont, carefully darkening ovals beside the senator's name, two blue dots in a red sea.

I am already climbing the stairs back to bed. Ohio won't go to Kerry, I know it won't. "Oh, God." I say to myself. "We've lost."

This is history repeating itself. In November 2000 the results of the national election were held up by a voting snafu in Florida engineered by the Republican Party. There, names were removed from voter registration lists, with African Americans, immigrants, and others with a history in the criminal system targeted. In addition, almost two million ballots were not counted because they were "spoiled" by a stray mark or some other technical reason. According to the U.S. Civil Rights Commission, about half of these were cast by black Americans. Inaccurate counts and failed machines further botched the results.

With Florida's electoral votes in question, the election went to the U.S. Supreme Court for a final decision. Although Vice-President Al Gore won the popular vote, a court with a majority of Republican-appointed judges decided that George W. Bush would be president.

I am in anguish over my country. I live in a country I don't love. I'm supposed to follow and honor a president I don't respect.

Outside, the entire country seems to be mourning. The wind is brutal, cutting, howling beneath a winter sky. My next-door neighbor calls to me, dejected, shaking his head, trashcan in hand, "Can you believe this?" Across the street, a neighbor who voted Democrat for the first time in her life has a bewildered look on her face. She waves. When I take the newspaper from the box even the headline is ominous: *Here We Go Again.*

All day ours is a nation not celebrating a new president.

In the months before the 2004 election, Raven and I worked hard to put Ohio Congressman Dennis Kucinich in the White House, because he opposed the Iraq "war" and called for the establishment of a Department of Peace; then, when Senator John Kerry won the Democratic nomination, we worked for him. We knocked on doors, gave talks, donated what money we could afford, sent postcards, made phone calls. We left our son at home and rode a bus to New York to protest the Republican National Convention's agenda. That summer and fall I kept thinking, "I'm in a damned battle. I'm a *soldier* and I don't even believe in fighting."

Now the national news lies bitter in my heart. "My son will be grown by the time we have another president," I think. "And what will become of our country? More importantly, if we lose our democracy, what are we?"

When I was yet a young woman, my love of nature funneled me toward a life of activism: How could I not defend the wild places where I learned so much and found great hope and comfort? I became an environmentalist because I could not stand idly by and watch the degradation, toxification, privatization, and destruction of nature. If society assumed that silence was consent, I would not be silent.

The more I learned, the more I comprehended that environmental destruction is intrinsically and logically connected to every brand of oppression on the planet; destruction of wildness is one of many forms of violence against this glorious experiment we call life. Every brand of social domination, including racism, objectification of women, subjugation of native peoples, militarization of men, classism, control over young people, and genocide, parallels—in theory, at least—the exploitation of nature.

I learned that the only true opposition to domination is refusal to participate in it, which means reimagining a life that has equality at its axis and attempting to live that life. Most likely opposition will also mean dissent. I came to understand that what I stood to lose by being quiet and complacent was greater than what I stood to lose by protesting.

In the early 1990s I lived for six months in a small village in Colombia, South America, a country whose population has been decimated by civil unrest in the twentieth century. There, as a teacher in Fusagasuga, I moved through rich, tropical days terrified on the one hand of revolutionaries and on the other of the Colombian government with its huge appetite. In Bogota foot soldiers with M16s patrolled the streets. One day, in the part of the country known as El Llano, the bus on which I was riding was halted by guerillas (or was it soldiers?) at a roadblock and all the passengers were ordered at gunpoint from the bus. One by one in the searing heat we were searched and after maybe an hour, not finding whatever they were looking for, the soldiers allowed us to continue on our way.

I remember a particularly beautiful, sunny afternoon in Fusagasuga's main square. A friend was visiting from the United States, and we sat with our backs to the cathedral and read aloud our American Bill of Rights, the first ten amendments to our Constitution, ratified on December 15, 1791. Around us doves cooed in stone niches.

I was stunned by what I read. Our country wasn't perfect, but compared to Colombia, where fear stained every moment, it was built on the rock of good intentions. It was off to a great start. We citizens of the United States of America have the incredible fortune to be born in a democratic country, one designed by forward-thinking people. We have rights. We can speak out.

In the days following the 2004 presidential election, civil rights attorneys and poll watchers found problems in Ohio that mirrored those in Florida in 2000. There were hundreds of cases of vote suppression, evident in long lines, waits of up to eight hours, failed machines, too few machines placed in poor neighborhoods, and computer glitches that strangely kept favoring Bush. It didn't help matters that the CEO of Diebold, one of the two largest voting machine companies, promised to deliver Ohio to Bush. As for other states, exit polls were off only in key swing states, but without a paper trail, recounts were impossible. "Correct Electile Dysfunction," demanded the radical leaflets.

I feel despair about what our country has become and is becoming.

We invaded Iraq for oil and allowed a so-called war to drag on for years. Not only were we presented trumped-up justifications for attacking Iraq in the first place, all redresses of government have been ignored systematically. On the last day of 2006 the Pentagon announced that the 3,000th soldier had died in Iraq; six months later the figure was 3,600. Sixty percent of those killed never reached their twenty-fifth birthday; most came from poor, rural areas. In addition to the U.S. service members, nearly 400 nonmilitary contractors were dead, as well as 6,000 members of the Iraqi military. Hundreds of thousands of Iraqi citizens had been killed. This is not to mention the wounded on all sides.

Dissenters are punished, beaten, marginalized, hushed, put in jail. Public protesters are relegated to "free-speech zones." The president, who goes to great lengths to avoid any signs of dissent, authorizes phones to be tapped, illegally, and not one judge calls him to task. The USA PATRIOT Act, which strips Americans of hard-earned rights, speeds through Congress, unread and undebated.

I have come to believe that we are experiencing a coup in our sweet country, not your normal political revolutionary takeover but a *corporate* coup. Its leaders will do almost anything to keep money flowing their way.

Corporations, using well-trained, well-paid, and conniving corporate lawyers as their agents, have step by step, decade by decade, moved the entire country toward a corporate state. We wake up and look around to find that we have evolved into a one-party system of government, the Business Party. Although we duly elect our representatives, their campaigns are funded by donations from corporations and the wealthy emissaries of corporations, until most of them, obligated to business interests, abandon the will of the people and the common good. Our politicians often are motivated by financial and political gain, not ethics, and support ideologies both hazardous to the people they represent and contrary to democracy.

The economic gap between the well-off and everybody else grows. Tax breaks blatantly enrich the upper class. Budgets for social programs are slashed. Education suffers. College tuition programs are cut, and students graduate from university tens of thousands of dollars in debt.

America's economic system is industrial, military capitalism. We Americans are great believers in the "free market," and we endlessly tout its benefits—it encourages risk, maximizes wealth, creates jobs, promotes efficiency. We were told and we believed that capitalism was the greatest economic system possible, that it would bring prosperity to every American and, as we globalized, to the poorest citizen of the poorest country in the world.

Now we know those claims to be grandly untrue. Capitalism destroys everything we love. In this country we have watched it fragment our families, communities, landscapes, environments, traditions, cultures, religions, and simple joys. In its heartless path we have lost our small farms, our farmers, our rivers, our prairies, our forests, our neighborhoods, our communities, our faiths. We have lost our souls. Facing the barrel of capitalism's gun we have been forced to accept violence, material culture, technology, sex hype, and war.

Capitalism is an unstoppable cancer that will grow and grow endlessly, and in the process will destroy even that which it depends on for survival. Meanwhile, we in the United States have imposed capitalism upon countries across the globe, and have set in motion a transnational fragmentation. Everywhere, the rich get richer and the poor poorer.

The word "corporation" never appears anywhere in our Constitution, yet, through a series of laws during the late nineteenth century, corporations have steadily gained influence in this country. The judiciary has allowed them to use laws meant to protect *people* to protect their existence and privilege. In fact, corporations have won more legal rights than people and freely use the people's military to protect those rights. An early victory for corporations came out of the 1886 case of *Santa Clara County v. Southern Pacific Railroad,* in which corporate attorneys argued that higher taxes for railroads were unconstitutional. In this case, they used the Fourteenth Amendment, which grants that no state shall "deny to any person . . . the equal protection of the laws." The U.S. Supreme Court ruled that a private corporation was a natural person and thus protected by the Constitution.

In later cases, corporations won the right to free speech and due process and security against unreasonable searches and seizures. Rights of personhood allowed corporations to influence legislation and gain access to courts.

Now, corporations run our government.

The door between industry and government revolves constantly. Lobbyists buy politicians. Lobbyists turn into politicians. Politicians become shareholders. Corporate lawyers press to privatize everything possible—our water, our educational system, our post, our Social Security. Top executives take us to war and profit handsomely. Politicians pass so-called "free trade" agreements that subvert national and international public-interest law.

Our democracy has slid into the hands of capitalists, whose bottom line is a dollar figure, and during the long, painful years of the Bush Administration this became clearer than ever before. Today

Americans are not so much citizens as consumers. Capitalism is slitting the throat of democracy. Our sweet country is in trouble.

And because of that, the world is in trouble, fragile and tender in the hands of the G-8, leaders of the eight most industrialized countries in the world, who control world finance, world peace, world poverty, world trade, world health, world war. "If globalization is the ultimate enclosure of the commons—our water, our biodiversity, our food, our culture, our health, our education—," wrote Indian thinker and activist Vandana Shiva, "then claiming the commons is the political, economic, and ecological agenda of our times."[1]

How can we save anything if we cannot save an individual's right to life, liberty, and pursuit of happiness? If human liberties fall away, how can we ever win rights for nonhumans, for wild places and wild creatures? How would we ever enfranchise the earth?

In 1987 the United Nations World Commission on Environment and Development called for a world charter that would set forth guiding principles of sustainable development. This charter became an item of business at the 1992 Earth Summit in Rio de Janeiro, but when the summit ended with the project unfinished, it languished. Two years later Maurice Strong, secretary general of the Earth Summit, enlisted Mikhail Gorbachev of Green Cross International to renew efforts to pen a document that would create a vision for the planet, and in 1997 a drafting committee was formed.

Unlike the Constitutional Convention of the United States, the committee sought ideas and opinions from all corners of the globe until finally, in 2000, the Earth Charter Commission approved a final version.

The Earth Charter, a brilliant and far-reaching document, puts into words a remarkable vision, "an ethical foundation for the emerging world community."[2] Powerfully succinct, the charter contains only four major tenets: Respect and Care for the Community of Life; Ecological Integrity; Social and Economic Justice; and Democracy, Nonviolence, and Peace.

Thus, the document recognizes democracy as a fundamental principle for a just, sustainable, and peaceful global society and challenges us to "Strengthen democratic institutions at all levels, and provide transparency and accountability in governance, inclusive participation in decision making, and access to justice."[3]

A few months ago I attended the weekend-long 130th Daniel Pennock Democracy School, taught by Ben Price of the Community Environmental Legal Defense Fund. CELDF, understanding that the federal government is in the grip of corporate control, aids communities in contesting corporate power at the local level. With its help and using a legal mandate called Home Rule, which allows municipalities the right to adopt charters, communities have passed ordinances that do such things as ban corporate agriculture within town limits or prevent corporations from withdrawing water from the ground and selling it for profit. Licking Township in Clarion County, Pennsylvania, even passed a rule "to eliminate the purported constitutional rights of corporations in order to remedy the harms that corporations may cause to the people of Licking Township."

Democracy School was named for Daniel Pennock, a seventeen-year-old who died of an infection from staphylococcus blown by the wind from land-applied sewage sludge. He was contaminated as he shot hoops in his backyard.

"Who makes the decisions?" asked Price. "If it's not the people affected by them, then it's not democracy. CELDF gives communities the power to say, 'This is our vision and we don't believe that factory farms (or whatever) fit into that vision.' Our intention is to create law that creates the kind of communities we want to live in."

An entire morning of Democracy School we spent defining democracy and tracing its roots in the United States. Americans, we learned, put great stock in the Constitution as the defining document of democracy worldwide. Yet upon examination we see that the Constitution was written by a group of white males, most of them lawyers who owned property. Women, African Americans, Native Americans, and poor people were excluded, except that a slave counted for representation as three-fifths of a person. During the closed-door 1787 Constitutional Convention in Philadelphia, delegates, who debated hotly the terms of the new government, were sworn to secrecy, and the papers from the convention weren't released until all attendees were dead.

In his 1893 talk before the American Historical Society meeting, Frederick Jackson Turner theorized that wilderness in America, more than any other force, helped birth our democracy. Although the United States was birthed in dissent and revolution, along the Atlantic coast wealthy industrialists and a planting aristocracy began to rise to dominance and to control the new continent. There was an easy remedy for this new oppression: the country's seemingly limitless frontier offered people a chance for a free life and a better livelihood, with success based on individual achievement. "On the frontier of New England, along the western border of Pennsylvania, Virginia, and the Carolinas, and in the communities beyond the Alleghany Mountains," wrote Turner, "there arose a demand of the frontier settlers for independent statehood based on democratic provisions." Where people had conquered "vacant lands" (in this case defined as void of European settlement) they won the right to establish political institutions of their choice.

"Who would rest content under oppressive legislative conditions," questioned Turner, "when with a slight effort he might reach a land wherein to become a co-worker in the building of free cities and free States on the lines of his own ideal?"[4]

It was these far-flung frontierspeople who opposed passage of the Constitution. They wanted self-governance and knew it couldn't be centralized. They feared that power given to a national government would be wielded by an upper class, eventually erasing the liberty of the common people. Jefferson, progenitor of our democracy, had arisen out of that frontier, as had Lincoln, who, in the first real test of U.S. democracy, granted emancipation to slaves.

The Constitution that was approved called for a legislative branch consisting of two houses, reminiscent of the Lords and Commons of Britain; for electing a president, an electoral college instead of a popular vote; senators chosen by state legislatures, not by the people (this changed); and no mention of rights. The Bill of Rights was added to appease states that complained, but even that document gave no new rights. As Ben Price pointed out, it simply protected the rights of those who already had them.

Later, after bitter campaigns, slavery was abolished and black Americans won the right to vote. "Our freedoms were not granted to us by any governments," Arundhati Roy said. "They were wrested from them by us."[5] (One cannot fail to be reminded that the Equal Rights Amendment was never ratified by Congress and therefore has never become part of our Constitution.)

The more I learned about democracy that weekend, the more I realized that our democracy is a baby one. It is fragile. The hour is early for freedom, justice a long way off.

Yet we've made a start. And the Earth Charter would move us forward. The Charter calls to "guarantee human rights and fundamental freedoms and provide everyone an opportunity to realize his or her full potential."[6] It gives rights to indigenous peoples, "to their spirituality, knowledge, lands and resources and to their related practice of sustainable livelihoods,"[7] to women as "equal partners, decision makers, leaders, and beneficiaries,"[8] and to young people who have a role in "creating sustainable societies."[9] The Earth Charter calls for the elimination of "discrimination in all its forms, such as that based on race, color, sex, sexual orientation, religion, language, and national, ethnic or social origin."[10] It calls for support of civil society, locally, regionally, and globally, and for "participation of all interested individuals and organizations in decision making."[11] The Earth Charter calls for the protection of "the rights to freedom of opinion, expression, peaceful assembly, association, and dissent."[12] The Earth Charter would "Eliminate corruption" and provide all people with "access to administrative and independent judicial procedures."[13] In its most far-reaching principles, the Earth Charter calls for the recognition that "all beings are interdependent and every form of life has value regardless of its worth to human beings" and for securing "Earth's bounty and beauty for present and future generations."[14]

Every morning my husband and I lie in bed a few minutes extra, trying to come to terms with the latest news. Torture, doubts about the explanation for what happened on September 11, 2001, and who was involved, climate disruption, trials. Daily, the number of dead in Iraq and Afghanistan grows. The amount of bad news is unreal. There are so many lies, and lies make us crazy because they negate intuition and good sense and science and reason.

My husband goes out for the paper and is reading headlines on his way back in.

"Bush is impeached?" I ask, facetiously and fractiously.

"Arctic Ice Melting."

I don't like having hate in my heart. At supper, we light candles for friends who are sick, for my baby niece whose mother smoked crack, for Mom's eye operation, for soldiers and families of soldiers. I start lighting another.

"For the softening of the president's heart," I say, touching flame to wick.

What are we to do? There seems to be only one good answer, and that is to do as the founders of our country did so well: revolt.

Vote. Perhaps make voting mandatory, so that more than forty percent of the population is electing leaders. Elect leaders based on majority vote. Put into place, as Burlington, Vermont, has done, instant runoff voting, where citizens rank candidates in order of preference, which allows voters to vote their conscience without "throwing their vote away." (For example, I believe people who voted for Nader in 2000 helped Gore lose the election.) We must ensure that all votes are counted—since honoring every vote is the first responsibility of a democracy—and that there's a paper record of every one. Outlaw electronic voting. Ban lobbyist gifts to politicians. Forbid corporations from making campaign contributions, and limit contributions by individuals. Run for public office ourselves.

Meanwhile, we watch other democracies around the world. We watch to see if Hugo Chavez is really going to distribute oil wealth to the people. We watch the Ukrainians in their Orange Revolution stand in the freezing cold for days for the right to fair elections. We watch Mexicans attempting the same. We watch the people of Bolivia take to the streets to protect water for the commons. "As the Bolivian people remind us," wrote Shiva, "there is one power stronger than the power of money and that's the power of people."[15]

Never forget that every right we have gained as citizens, every inch we have moved toward peace and justice and equality, every success we've had in protecting those beings that have no voice has been accompanied by struggle, by courage, and by someone holding up a vision so that people could walk toward it.

On an extravagantly sunny day in March 2006 I am sitting in Newfane, Vermont's town hall, built in 1832. It is town meeting day, when the residents of towns gather to act as a legislative body, one of the last examples of participatory democracy.

Along one gray wall is a row of voting booths, their half-curtains striped red, white, and blue, and people keep entering and exiting the booths while, on the floor, a meeting progresses. At the back of the room a bake sale benefits the sixth grade class trip to Montreal.

About 150 people are in the room, seventy percent of them gray-haired.

Town business includes an unfinished sidewalk, repair of the covered bridge, and high-speed Internet access for the village. Finally it is time for article 27. A reporter arrives.

The motion is a resolution to impeach the president.

People begin to speak, one testimony after another: a nephew who stood in line eight hours to vote in Ohio, thousands dead in Iraq, no weapons of mass destruction. Someone wants to add Karl Rove's name to the resolution. Others are scandalized. One wants to make sure that everyone speaking and voting on the resolution is a registered voter of Newfane, that outsiders haven't been brought in. Another wants to postpone the article.

Someone on the balcony is recognized by the moderator. "One of the unfortunate things about bringing national politics to town meeting is that it's very divisive," he says. "But even when we disagree, we can respect each other's opinions."

"This is civil debate. I'm very proud to be part of this town," says another.

"Chances are what we're doing is largely symbolic," someone says. "And what a hell of a symbol."

A vote is called, and a motion is made to use paper ballots. While the votes are being counted, the room is as silent as a bell jar. I'm in a movie, only it isn't a movie. The silence is history being made. The silence is the reality of American pain.

Finally the town moderator, wearing his black suit coat, stands and announces: *151 votes cast. 1 spoiled, 29 no, 121 yes.*

Despite the odds, I have hope for American democracy—at town meetings (the day's a state holiday in Vermont), at select-board and commission meetings, in committees. In 2006 a grassroots campaign made Bernie Sanders the first Socialist ever to take a seat in the U.S. Senate, even though Sanders was running against multimillionaire Rich Tarrant, who spent millions on high-priced television attack ads.

There's more hope. I know my state representatives by face and by name, and when I telephone them, we engage in real conversation.

By summer of 2007, forty Vermont towns had passed impeachment resolutions. When the Vermont Legislature took up the impeachment issue, since proceedings can come from any state as well as from Congress, over four hundred people flooded the statehouse to rally for it. Although the measure failed, it offered hope.

Via Democracy Schools, communities are protecting themselves from corporate atrocity. That's more hope.

I cannot speak for all Americans but this is my reality: I love my country, but I love democracy more.

NOTES

1. Vandana Shiva. *Earth Democracy: Justice, Sustainability, and Peace.* Cambridge, Mass.: South End Press, 2005.

2. Earth Charter, Preamble, paragraph 6.

3. Earth Charter, Principle 13.

4. Frederick Jackson Turner. *The Frontier in American History.* New York: Henry Holt, 1920. Chapter 9, Contributions of the West to American Democracy.

5. Arundhati Roy. From "Instant-Mix Imperial Democracy: Buy One, Get One Free." Talk given at the Riverside Church, Harlem, May 13, 2003.

6. Earth Charter, Subprinciple 3a.

7. Earth Charter, Subprinciple 12b.
8. Earth Charter, Subprinciple 11b.
9. Earth Charter, Subprinciple 12c.
10. Earth Charter, Subprinciple 12a.
11. Earth Charter, Subprinciple 13b.
12. Earth Charter, Subprinciple 13c.
13. Earth Charter, Subprinciple 13e and 13d.
14. Earth Charter, Subprinciple 1a and Principle 4.
15. Vandana Shiva. *Earth Democracy: Justice, Sustainability, and Peace.* Cambridge, Mass.: South End Press, 2005.

Imagination and Principle into a New Ethic

The Ethic of Care

Leonardo Boff
Translated by Philip Berryman

Among so many other fine things, the Earth Charter proposes a new *way of seeing* that gives rise to a new *ethic*. The new way of seeing is understanding the inter- and retro-connections of all with all, for "Our environmental, economic, political, social, and spiritual challenges are interconnected, and together we can forge inclusive solutions."[1] Likewise, the new *ethic*, consistent with the new way of seeing, is based on the four creative energies of ecologically healthy human reality, called Parts in the Earth Charter, namely: (1) respect and care for the community of life; (2) ecological integrity; (3) social and economic justice; and (4) democracy, nonviolence, and peace.

The effect of these four interdependent principles, when reflected in society and culture, is "a sustainable way of life."[2] This sustainable way of life is equivalent to happiness in traditional versions of ethics deriving from the Greek, medieval, and modern traditions. The supreme value now, that which must save the system of life, of humankind, and of Earth, comes under the sign of care. It represents the new collective dream of humankind. The Earth Charter has given it a name: a sustainable way of life.

The new dream: A sustainable way of life

A sustainable way of life entails much more than "sustainable development," a key expression in official documents of governments and multilateral agencies, whose meaning is expanded by the Earth

Charter.[3] A sustainable way of life is humankind's new ethical and cultural dream. It entails another way of conceiving the common future of Earth and humankind and, accordingly, it demands a true revolution in minds and hearts, values and habits, forms of production, and relationship with nature. It entails understanding that "Humanity is part of a vast evolving universe" and that "Earth, our home, is alive"[4]; it also entails living "the spirit of human solidarity and kinship with all life," and assuming "responsibility for the present and the future well-being of the human family and the larger living world,"[5] taking care to use the scarce goods of nature rationally so as not to do harm to natural capital or to future generations who also have a right to a good quality of life and minimally just institutions, "being more, not having more"[6] and living "with reverence for the mystery of being, gratitude for the gift of life, and humility regarding the human place in nature."[7]

As is evident, this sustainable way of life demands a new human being, creating a new history different from that which humans have constructed thus far. Only through this sustainable way of life can we respond "together in hope"[8] to the challenges of life and death that we face.

The Preamble opens with an extremely important finding, one that prompted the creation of the Earth Charter: "We stand at a critical moment in Earth's history, a time when humanity must choose its future"[9] and "form a global partnership to *care* for Earth and one another or risk the destruction of ourselves and the diversity of life"[10] (emphasis added). the Preamble states: "The foundations of global security are threatened."[11]

These statements are not at all alarmist. They reveal the true crossroads that humankind has reached. It has created the principle of its own self-destruction with analytic reason and the project of technoscience used to dominate nature and persons. With biological, chemical, and nuclear weapons we can wreak profound havoc with the biosphere and block the planetary human project, conceivably even ending the human species, *homo sapiens* and *demens*.[12]

Thus far we foolishly allowed ourselves to cut down forests, pollute the atmosphere, contaminate waters, and wage wars with conventional weapons. We were operating under the assumption that natural resources were infinite and renewable, and that life and Earth would continue endlessly toward the future. That assumption is illusory. Resources are not infinite—and the earth can be completely wiped out.[13] Militarily powerful nations can carry out shameful wars against weaker countries. But they cannot do so with those that have weapons of mass destruction. It would be the end of civilization, perhaps of the human future itself. Hence either we care for the inheritance received from fifteen billion years of cosmic work, and 3.8 billion years of biotic activity, or we could share the fate of the dinosaurs who, in a short period of time, disappeared sixty-seven million years ago, after reigning supreme on the face of the Earth for over 130 million years.

In other words, humanity and Earth stand together facing the future. This future is not guaranteed by the forces leading the universe. We have to want it. Hence the Earth Charter goes on to say realistically "we must decide to live with a sense of universal responsibility."[14] Accordingly, the principle of self-destruction must be counteracted with the principle of care and of universal coresponsibility.

If the Earth Charter calls attention to these risks it also points to potential opportunities. In the spirit of the Earth Charter, the scenario is one of crisis, not tragedy. And every crisis is purifying and refining. It offers the chance of great changes and of the emergence of a higher and better order. "[G]reat peril, and great promise". . . "These trends are perilous—but not inevitable" the Preamble rightly proclaims.[15]

This is the context in which the ethic of care proposed by the Earth Charter gains relevance as one of the axes around which the sustainable way of life revolves. It will either be oriented by care or it will not be sustainable.[16]

Care and its echoes in the Earth Charter

The Earth Charter speaks of *care* four times, always in important contexts: "to *care* for Earth and one another"[17]; "Respect and *Care* for the Community of Life"[18]; "*Care* for the community of life with understanding, compassion, and love"[19]; and "to *care* for their environments"[20] (emphasis added).

But echoes of care or similar terms permeate the entire text. Categories correlated with care, such as "sustainability" and "responsibility," are especially prominent. Sustainability is predicated not only on development, but on a "way of life,"[21] "life,"[22] "livelihood,"[23] "society,"[24] and "global community."[25] Responsibility is "universal" and "to one another."[26] The term "concern" is likewise used for the global environment in the Preamble and Principle 5. Elsewhere the Earth Charter speaks of "preserving a healthy biosphere"[27] or it encourages us to "preserve our natural heritage."[28] The Earth Charter also seeks to protect, and calls to "protect . . . the integrity" of nature[29] or of natural reserves[30] or even safeguarding "Earth's regenerative capacities."[31] It also speaks of "applying a precautionary approach"[32] and urges preventing harm to the environment.[33]

We want to concentrate on the category of "care" because of its inner riches.[34] Care and sustainability are, we believe, the central categories of the new planetary paradigm. They are also the two principles that can make possible a globalized society and allow for a development that meets human needs and those of other beings in the biotic community. Such development can likewise preserve nature's integrity, beauty, and regenerative capacity with its resources for the sake of generations to come. That is what sustainability means.[35]

What is care? When does it arise? What is its function in the life process? How is an ethic based on care structured?

The fable of care and its implications

There is no better way to approach an understanding of care than the well-known fable number 220 of Hyginus (43 BCE–17 CE), a freedman who served Caesar Augustus as his librarian and philosopher. The fable goes like this:

> Once when "Care" was crossing a river she saw some clay; she thoughtfully took up a piece and began to shape it. While she was meditating on what she had made, Jupiter came by. "Care" asked

> him to give it spirit and this he gladly granted. But when she wanted her name to be bestowed upon it, he forbade this, and demanded that it be given his name instead. While "Care" and Jupiter were disputing, Earth arose and desired that her own name be conferred on the creature, since she had furnished it with part of her body. They asked Saturn to be their arbiter, and he made the following decision, which seemed a just one: "Since you, Jupiter, have given its spirit, you shall receive that spirit at its death; and since you, Earth, have given its body, you shall receive its body. But since 'Care' first shaped this creature, she shall possess it as long as it lives. And because there is now a dispute among you as to its name, let it be called 'homo' for it is made out of *humus* (earth)."[36]

This fable is filled with anthropological and ecological implications. Most importantly, care is prior to the spirit infused by Jupiter and prior to the body provided by Earth. The conception of body and spirit is accordingly not primordial. What is primordial is care, which "first shaped" the human being. Care did so with "care," zeal, and devotion, and thus with a loving attitude.

Care is the ontological *a priori*, that which must exist previously for the human being to emerge. Care is therefore at the core of the human being's makeup. Without it the human would not exist. Care thus constitutes the real and true essence of the human being. Hence, as the fable says, care "shall possess" the human being "as long as it lives." Whatever humans do with care will reveal us as we are.

The psychoanalyst Rollo May rightly says: "Our situation is that in our heyday of rationalistic and technicalistic episodes, we have lost sight of and concern for the human being; and we must now humbly go back to the simple fact of care. . . . It is the mythos of care—and that mythos alone—which enables us to stand against the cynicism and apathy which are the psychological illnesses of our day."[37]

Care in cosmogenesis and biogenesis

If we think about it, care is not just a category that defines who human beings, man and woman, are, but it also enables us to understand the universe. Care is as ancestral as the cosmos in evolution.

If, after the Big Bang, there had been no care on the part of the guiding forces by which the universe creates itself and regulates itself—that is, the gravitational and electromagnetic forces, and the weak and strong nuclear forces—everything would have expanded too much, preventing matter from condensing and forming the universe as we know it. Or everything would have been pulled in to the point where the universe would collapse upon itself in interminable explosions, preventing the formation of ordered matter. But it didn't. Everything proceeded with a care so subtle, in such a "careful" balance, of fractions of billionths of seconds, as calculated by cosmologists Steven Weinberg and Stephen Hawking, that it allowed us to be here and to talk about all these things.[38]

Care gained further momentum when life emerged 3.8 billion years ago. With utterly singular care, the first bacteria engaged in chemical dialogue with their environment to assure their survival and evolution.

Care acquired further complexity with the emergence of mammals, from which we have come, 125 million years ago, bringing with them the limbic brain, the organ of emotion, care, and tenderness.

Care gained centrality with the emergence of human beings, seven million years ago. Care is their underlying structure on which is built their essence, as in the lesson of the fable examined above.

We exist only because our mothers cared for us even in their wombs. And when we were born, they provided us with complete care, in an unconditional act of generosity and love. It was the extraordinary English pediatrician and psychoanalyst Donald W. Winnicott (1896–1962) who showed the fundamental importance of motherly care in the constitution of the basic psychological structures of the child, structures that will define its ethical direction, and its relationship to otherness.[39]

Care is that *a priori* condition that allows for the explosion of intelligence and loving; it goes before all behavior, guiding it to be free and responsible, and, in short, characteristically human. Care is loving gesture toward reality, gesture that protects and brings tranquility and peace. Care is always essential care.

No living thing survives without care. Care is the stronger force that stands up to the law of entropy, the natural wearing-out of all things, because everything for which we care lasts much longer.

Today we must rescue this attitude as a minimal and universal ethic if we want to preserve that inheritance that we receive from the universe and from culture and assure our common future.

Care and cultural crises

History has shown us that whenever crisis situations break out, care also emerges in consciousness. Let us simply put forth some illustrative instances that prove how right the Earth Charter is in choosing care as a core category for establishing a sustainable way of life.

Florence Nightingale (1820–1910) is the archetype of the modern nurse. In 1854 she set out with thirty-eight colleagues from London to a military hospital in Turkey, where the Crimean War was being fought. Imbued with the idea of care, she succeeded in reducing mortality from forty-two percent to two percent in two months.

World War I destroyed certainties and produced a deep metaphysical helplessness. That was when Martin Heidegger (1889–1976) wrote his brilliant *Being and Time* (1927), whose central sections (§§ 39–44) are devoted to care as ontology of the human being.[40] There he says, "care as a primary structural reality, lies 'before' ('*vor*') every factical 'attitude' and 'situation' of Dasein, and it does so existentially *a priori*; this means that it always lies in them" (§ 42). Care must be understood in the line of human essence. It responds to the question, "What is the human being?" By the very fact of being human, the human being is essentially a being of care. Formalizing the essential understanding Heidegger says "with the expression 'care' we have in mind a basic existential ontological phenomenon" (§ 42).

In 1972, the Club of Rome, a global think tank and center of innovation, sounded the ecological alarm on Earth's sickly condition. It identified the main cause, our pattern of predatory, wasteful, consumerist development. Sustainable development was proposed as the solution.

The United Nations Environment Programme, the World Wildlife Fund, and the World Conservation Union drew up a detailed strategy for the future of the Planet under the title "Caring for the Earth" (1991). It states: "The ethic of care applies at the international as well as the national and individual levels. All nations stand to gain from worldwide sustainability and are threatened if we fail to attain it."[41]

Drawing on this tradition, the drafting of the Earth Charter was completed in March 2000 and UNESCO accepted it on that same date. It is the text of the new ecological and ethical conscience of humankind in which the category of care occupies a central place.

Francis of Assisi, Mahatma Gandhi, Aldo Leopold, Mother Teresa of Calcutta, and Chico Mendes have all been marked by care, as have so many men and women, starting with our mothers, sisters, and grandparents. They are archetypes who inspire the path of care and of rescuing life and Earth.

We now want to comment on Principle 2 of Part I, Respect and Care for the Community of Life, which reads: "Care for the community of life with understanding, compassion, and love."[42] Let us examine each part.

Care for the community of life with understanding

Caring means being involved with the other or with the community of life showing zeal and indeed concern. But it is always an attitude of goodwill that wishes to be alongside, to accompany, and to protect. Understanding seeks to know the community of life emotionally. It wants to know with the heart and not simply the head. Hence, it is not at all about knowing in order to dominate (knowledge is power for moderns like Francis Bacon) but knowing in order to enter into communion with reality.[43] For that we need what Blaise Pascal calls "*esprit de finesse*" as opposed to the "*esprit de géometrie*." The spirit of kindness and courtesy grasps others as other, seeks to understand their inner logic and accept them as they are. This understanding entails love and goodwill and overcoming malice and suspicion. Saint Augustine rightly said, in Plato's wake, "we know insofar as we love."

Caring for the community of life with understanding thus means using science and technology always in consonance with this community, never against it, or sacrificing its integrity and beauty. Caring here is an invitation to ecologize everything we do with the community of life, that is, to refuse interactions that are harmful to ecosystems or that cause suffering to the representatives of the community of life as the Earth Charter urges in Principle 15: "Treat all living beings with respect and consideration"; it means maintaining the intermingling of beings, avoiding monocultures, and uniform thinking, so that the logic of inclusion and the holistic perspective prevails.[44]

Care for the community of life with compassion

In order to properly understand compassion, we must first devote some attention to our language, for in everyday understanding this word has pejorative connotations that rob it of its highly positive content. In everyday understanding, having compassion means "having pity" on the other, a feeling that lowers him or her to the condition of someone bereft of his or her own potentiality and inner energy to stand up. We suffer with such a person and share the pain of his or her situation.

We could also understand compassion in the sense of paleo-Christianity (primordial Christianity, before it took the form of churches) as synonym of mercy, a highly positive sense.[45] Having mercy (*miseri-cór-dia*) means having a heart (*cor*) that can feel the poor (*míseros*) and emerge from self to aid them. That stance is suggested by the very philology of the word com-passion: sharing the passion of others and *with* others, suffering *with* them, rejoicing *with* them, walking the path *with* them. But this meaning has not prevailed in history. What has prevailed is the moralistic lesser sense of one who looks down from above and dispenses alms into the hand of the sufferer. Showing mercy comes to mean doing "charity" to the other, charity thus criticized by the Argentine singer and poet Atahualpa Yupanqui: "I have contempt for charity because of the shame wrapped in it. / I am like the mountain lion who lives and dies alone."[46]

The Buddhist conception of compassion is different, however. Compassion may be one of the greatest ethical contributions that the East offers humankind. Compassion has to do with the basic question that gave rise to Buddhism as an ethical and spiritual path.

The question is: what is the best means to free us from suffering? The Buddha's answer is: "through compassion, through infinite compassion."

The Dalai Lama updates this time-honored reply as follows: "help others whenever you can, and if you cannot, never harm them."[47] This understanding is in line with the unconditional love and forgiveness proposed by Jesus.

The "great compassion" (*karuna* in Sanskrit) entails two attitudes: *detachment* from all beings in the community of life and *care* for all of them. By *detachment* we distance ourselves from them, relinquishing possession of them and learning to respect them in their otherness and difference. Through *care* we approach beings to enter into communion with them, accepting responsibility for their well-being and aiding them in their suffering.

We have here a behavior in solidarity that has nothing to do with pity and mere handout "charity." To Buddhists, the level of detachment reveals the degree of freedom and maturity that the person has reached. And the level of care shows how much goodwill and responsibility the person has developed toward the whole community of life and toward everything in the universe. Compassion encompasses two dimensions. Hence it demands freedom, altruism, and love.

The ethos that shows compassion knows no limits. The Buddhist ideal is the *bodhisattva,* that person who takes the ideal of compassion so far that he or she is willing to give up nirvana and even to agree to go through an infinite number of lives solely in order to help others in their suffering. This altruism is expressed in the *Prayer of the Bodhisattva*:

> As long as space abides
> and as long as sentient beings remain,
> May I too abide
> and dispel the sufferings of beings.[48]

Tibetan culture expresses this ideal through the figure of the Buddha with a thousand arms and two thousand eyes. With them, in compassion, it can serve an unlimited number of people.

From the Buddhist standpoint, the ethos that shows compassion teaches us how our relationship to the community of life ought to be: respect it in its otherness, live with it as a member, and care for it, and especially regenerate those beings that suffer or are threatened with extinction. Only then should we make use of their gifts, in a fair proportion, for what we need to live adequately and decently.

Care for the community of life with love

Love is the greatest force in the universe, in living beings, and in humans. For love is a force of attraction, union, and transfiguration. The ancient Greek myth formulated it as follows: Eros, the god of life, rose up to create the Earth. Before, everything was silence, naked and immobile. Now everything is life, joy, movement. Love is the highest expression of care because everything we love we also care for. And everything we care for is a sign that we also love.

Humberto Maturana, one of the greatest exponents of contemporary biology, has shown in his studies of *autopoiesis*, that is, on the self-organization of matter which issues in life, how love emerges from within the cosmic process.[49] In nature, says Maturana, are found two kinds of linkages, those of beings with the environment and those with each other. One is *necessary*, linked to the very subsistence of beings, and the other is *spontaneous*, connected to gratuitous relations, for sheer pleasure, in the flow of life itself. When this happens, even at very early stages of evolution, billions of years ago, love emerges as a cosmic and biological phenomenon. As the universe expands and becomes complex, this spontaneous loving linkage tends to increase. In human beings, it gains strength and becomes the primary motive of human actions. It was this relationship of loving and care that allowed our hominid and anthropoid ancestors to make the leap toward humanity. When they went out to gather food and hunt, they did not eat by themselves but brought their food to the group where they shared in a family spirit among everyone, likewise expressing their feelings. Language itself, which is characteristic of human beings, arose within this dynamism of love and mutual care.

Love is always oriented to the Other. It always means an Abrahamitic adventure, that of leaving one's own reality and going out to meet what is different and establishing a relationship of covenant, friendship, and love with it. It is the birthplace of ethics.[50]

The irruption of the Other in my face is the beginning of ethics. For the Other forces me to take a practical stance, of welcome, of indifference, of rejection, of destruction. The Other signifies a proposal, which asks for a response with responsibility (*pro-posta, res-posta, res-ponsa-bilidade*).

The most onerous limit of the Western paradigm has to do with the Other, for whom it does not reserve any special place.[51] Indeed, it does not know what to do with the Other, whom it has either absorbed, brought under submission, or destroyed. This also applies to the community of life. The West has embodied a rigid anthropocentrism that has not allowed room for the otherness of nature. The relationship was not of communion and inclusion, but of exploitation and submission. By denying the Other, it has lost the chance for covenant and mutual learning. The paradigm of identity without difference has prevailed, following in the wake of the pre-Socratic Parmenides.

The Other causes the emergence of the ethos of loving. Paradigmatic of this ethos is the Christianity of origin, paleo-Christianity. It is distinguished from the Christianity of history and its churches, which in its ethics has been more influenced by the Greek masters than by the message and practice of Jesus. By contrast, paleo-Christianity gives absolute centrality to love of the Other, which for Jesus is the same as love for God. Love is so central that one who has love has all. It witnesses to this sacred conviction that God is love (1 John 4:8), love comes from God (1 John 4:7), and love will never die (1 Cor. 13:8). This love is unconditional and universal, for it encompasses even the enemy (Luke 6:35). The loving ethos is expressed in the golden rule, attested by all human traditions: "Love your neighbor as yourself"; "Do not do to the other what you do not want done to you."

Love is thus central because for Christianity the Other is central. Indeed God became other, through the incarnation. Without going by way of the Other, without the "more other" Other, i.e., the one who is hungry, poor, a pilgrim, or naked, God cannot be found, nor can fullness of life (Matt. 25:31–46) be attained. This going out of self toward others to love them in themselves, to love them without return, unconditionally, lays the groundwork for the most inclusive possible ethos, the most humanizing ethos imaginable. This love is a single movement; it goes out to the other, to the community of life, and to God.

No one in the West has become an archetype of this loving and heartfelt ethos more than Saint Francis of Assisi. He united the two ecologies, internal ecology (by integrating his emotions and desires) and external ecology (by establishing kinship with all beings). Eloi Leclerc, one of the best contemporary Franciscan thinkers, a survivor of the Nazi death camps at Buchenwald, observes:

> Rather than hardening himself and becoming enclosed in proud isolation, he allowed himself to be despoiled of everything, to become tiny, to take his place very humbly, in the midst of creatures, a neighbor to the most humble among them. He established kinship with Earth itself, with its original soil, with its obscure roots. And indeed, "our sister and Mother-Earth" opened before his marveling eyes a path of unlimited borderless brother- and sisterhood. A kinship that embraced all creation. Humble Francis became the brother of the Sun, the stars, the wind, the clouds, water, fire, and everything living.[52]

This is the result of an essential love that embraces the whole community of life with affection, tenderness, and love.

The loving ethos lays the groundwork for giving life new meaning. Loving the Other, whether the human being or each representative of the community of life, means giving it a reason for being. There is no reason for existing. Existence is sheer gratuity. Loving the Other means wanting the Other to exist because love makes the other important. Love is saying to another: you will not die, you must exist, you cannot die.

When someone or something becomes important to the Other, a value that mobilizes all vital energies appears. That is why when people love they are rejuvenated and have the sensation that they are beginning life anew. Love is the source of values.

Only this loving ethos can measure up to the challenges we face in the community of life, which finds itself devastated and threatened and futureless. This love respects otherness, opens up to it, and seeks a communion that enriches all. It brings close those who are afar, and makes brothers and sisters of those who are nearby.

Conclusion: Care and the future of life

If life can arise in a context of care, it is through ongoing care, through all the time in which it will exist on the face of the Earth, that life maintains itself, reproduces itself, and coevolves. Today we understand that the revolution of care has become imperative. As care belongs to the essence of the human being, it must serve as a minimum consensus on which a planetary ethic can be based, an ethic that everyone can understand and everyone can practice.[53]

In one of his songs the black Brazilian poet and singer Milton Nascimento sang: "há que se cuidar do broto para que a vida nos dê flor e fruto" (the seedling must be cared for so that life may give us flower and fruit). That applies to Earth and all ecosystems: we have to "care with understanding, compassion, and love" for Earth, understood as Gaia, Magna Mater, and the Pacha Mama of our indigenous peoples, so that she can secure her vitality, integrity, and beauty. We—Earth and Humankind—comprise a single entity, as the astronauts have been thrilled to see from their spacecraft out there in space. From that vantage point, there is no difference between Earth and Humankind. Both make up a single entity with a single origin and a single destiny. Only care will assure the sustainability of the Earth-system with all beings of the community of life, among which is situated the human being, one axis among others, of this vast current of life. Humankind's function is that of gardener, as portrayed in Genesis, chapter 2. The gardener's work is to care for the Garden of Eden, to make it fruitful and beautiful. The Earth Charter has awakened us, just in time, to this essential and urgent mission of ours.

NOTES

1. Earth Charter, Preamble, paragraph four.

2. Earth Charter, Preamble, paragraph six.

3. Sustainable development is discussed in detail in L. Boff, *Ecology and Liberation: A New Paradigm* (Maryknoll, N.Y.: Orbis Books, 1995) and *Cry of the Earth, Cry of the Poor* (Maryknoll, N.Y.: Orbis Books, 1998).

4. Earth Charter, Preamble, paragraph two.

5. Earth Charter, Preamble, paragraph five.

6. Earth Charter, Preamble, paragraph four.

7. Earth Charter, Preamble, paragraph five.

8. Earth Charter, Preamble, paragraph six.

9. Earth Charter, Preamble, paragraph one.

10. Earth Charter, Preamble, paragraph four.

11. Earth Charter, Preamble, paragraph three.

12. See L. Boff, *Do iceberg à arca de Noé: o nascimento de uma ética planetária* (Rio de Janeiro: Garamond, 2002).

13. See, for example, D. Toolan, *At Home in the Cosmos* (Maryknoll, N.Y.: Orbis Books, 2001), part III, The State of the Earth, 75–125.

14. Earth Charter, Preamble, paragraph five.

15. Earth Charter, Preamble, paragraph three.

16. On the "ethic of care" see B. R. Hill, *Christian Faith and the Environment* (Maryknoll, N.Y.: Orbis Books, 1998); J. R. Des Jardins, *Environmental Ethics* (Belmont, Calif.: Wadsworth, 1977); A. Auer, *Umweltethik* (Düsseldorf: Patmos, 1985); and P. Schmitz, *Ist die Schöpfung noch zu retten?* (Würzburg: Echter, 1995).

17. Earth Charter, Preamble, paragraph four.

18. Earth Charter, Part 1.

19. Earth Charter, Principle 2.

20. Earth Charter, Subprinciple 13f.

21. Earth Charter, Preamble, paragraph six.

22. Earth Charter, Principle 5.

23. Earth Charter, Subprinciple 9b.

24. Earth Charter, Subprinciple 12c.

25. Earth Charter, The Way Forward, paragraph four.

26. Earth Charter, Preamble, paragraph one.

27. Earth Charter, Preamble, paragraph two.

28. Earth Charter, Subprinciple 5b.

29. Earth Charter, Principle 5.

30. Earth Charter, Subprinciples 5b, 12b, and 15b.

31. Earth Charter, Principle 7.

32. Earth Charter, Principle 6.

33. Earth Charter, Principle 6, Subprinciple 5d.

34. See the following primary bibliography: L. Boff, *Saber cuidar: ética do humano, compaixão pela Terra* (Petrópolis: Vozes, 1999); F. Torralba y Roselló, *Antropología del cuidar* (Barcelona: Fundación Mapfre Medicina, 1998); V. R. Waldow, *Cuidado humano—resgate necessário* (Porto Alegre: Sagra Luzzatto, 1998); S. T. Fry, *A Global Agenda for Caring* (New York: National League for Nursing Press, 1993), 175–79; S. T. Fry, "The Philosophical Foundations of Caring," in M. M. Leininger (ed.), *Ethical and Moral Dimensions of Care* (Detroit: Wayne State University Press, 1990); M. M. Leininger and J. Watson, *The Caring Imperative in Education* (New York: Nation League for Nursing, 1990); M. Mayeroff, *On Caring* (New York: Harper Perennial, 1971); J. M. Morse et al. "Concepts of Caring and Caring as a Concept," *Advances in Nursing Science*, vol. 13, n. 1, p. 1–14, 1990; N. Noddings, *Caring: A Feminine Approach to Ethics and Moral Education* (Berkeley: University of California Press, 1984); P. L., Chinn, *Anthology on Caring* (New York: Nation League of Nursing Press, 1991); M. J., dos S. Rossi, "O curar and o cuidar—a história de uma relação," *Revista Brasileira de Enfermagem* (Brasília), vol. 44, n. 1, 16–21, 1991.

35. On sustainability, see the classic, R. Goodland et al., *Medio ambiente y desarrollo sostenible. Más allá del informe Brundtland* (Madrid: Trotta, 1992).

36. Translated from Latin in Martin Heidegger, *Being and Time* (San Francisco: HarperSanFrancisco, 1962), 242.

37. Rollo May, *Love and Will* (New York: Dell, 1969), 202, 203.

38. On the careful balance, see Steven Weinberg, *The First Three Minutes Os três primeiros minutos. Uma análise moderna da origem do universo* (Lisboa: Gradiva, 1987), and Stephen Hawking, *A Brief History of Time: From the Big Bang to Black Holes* (New York: Bantam, 1988).

39. Donald W. Winnicott, "Dependence in Infant Care, Child Care, Psychoanalytic Setting," *International Journal of Psychoanalysis*, vol. 44, 1963, 338–344; Winnicott, *Mother and Child: A Primer of First Relationship* (New York: Basic Books, 1957); Winnicott, *Human Nature* (New York: Schocken, 1988).

40. Heidegger, *Being and Time*, 238.

41. International Union for Conservation of Nature and Natural Resources, *Caring for the Earth: A Strategy for Sustainable Living* (Gland, Switzerland: IUCN [the World Conservation Union, UN Environment Programme, World Wide Fund for Nature], 1991).

42. Earth Charter, Principle 2.

43. Cf. J. Moltmann, "Die Entdeckung der Anderen. Zur Theorie des kommunikativen Erkennes," *Evangelische Theologie*, n.5, 1990, 400–414.

44. J. B. McDaniel, *With Roots and Wings* (Maryknoll, N.Y.: Orbis Books, 1995).

45. Matthew Fox, *A Spirituality Named Compassion and the Healing of the Global Village, Humpty Dumpty, and Us* (San Francisco: Harper & Row, 1990); J. Sobrino, *The Principle of Mercy: Taking the Crucified People from the Cross* (Maryknoll, N.Y.: Orbis Books, 1994).

46. The lyric is from Atahualpa Yupanqui's "Milonga." The original is "Desprecio la caridad, / por la vergüenza que encierra. / Soy como el león de las sierras: / ¡vivo y muero en soledad!"

47. Dalai Lama, *The Good Heart: A Buddhist Perspective on the Teachings of Jesus* (Boston: Wisdom Publications, 1996), 170.

48. Ibid., 219; Dalai Lama, *Ethics for the New Millennium* (New York: Riverhead Books, 1999).

49. On love emerging from within the cosmic process, see *A ontologia da realidade* (Belo Horizonte: Editora da UFMG, 1997); *A árvore do conhecimento: As bases biológicas do entendimento humano* (Campinas: Psy II, 1995); together with F. Varela, *De máquinas and seres vivos. Autopoiese—a organização do ser vivo* (Porto Alegre: Artes Médicas, 1997).

50. L. Boff, *Etica e Moral. Fundamentos* (Petrópolis: Vozes, 2003).

51. See the classic D. de Rougemont, *L'amour et l'Occident* (Paris: Librairie Plon, 1972). Published in English as *Love in the Western World* (New York: Pantheon, 1956).

52. E. Leclerc, *Le soleil se lève sur Assise* (Paris: Desclée de Brouwer, 1999), 124.

53. L. Boff, *Ethos mundial. Um consenso mínimo entre os humanos* (Rio de Janeiro: Sextante, 2003).

Afterword

Kamla Chowdhry

Historically, when humanity reaches new lows, someone or something happens. With the despair and degradation that accompanied colonialism, Gandhi happened in India and Nelson Mandela happened in South Africa. Both Gandhi and Mandela changed the map of the world. With the rise of industrialization and globalization, our society as a whole is in deep crisis. We read about the many manifestations of industrialization and globalization in the papers. Besides the mutilation and degradation of Earth, there is high unemployment, high poverty, high corruption, high pollution, high crime, and high suicide rates. The way we have used our science and technology has been severely disturbing. We need new visionaries with a new way of seeing and defining progress and development.

In the last two or three decades, new visionaries Maurice Strong happened and Mikhail Gorbachev happened. They have helped initiate new thinking, new institutions, and new ecological awareness; they are helping in the moral and spiritual transition that is necessary for developing a new framework of sustainable development. From them, as from others, we are learning that there can be no sustainable development or sustainable future without morality and compassion and spirituality. Most changes that have altered the course of history have begun with individuals like Strong and Gorbachev, who by their example and actions did what many thought impossible. Underlying each one is a moral conviction and a fearlessness that refuses to be subdued.

The Earth Charter makes an appeal to humanity to move in the direction of sustainable living, of moral and ethical living, of compassionate and peaceful living, of enlightened living, and of pursuing technological change with a human face. How should we act, and how should we move toward sustainable and enlightened living? The Earth Charter is an attempt to answer these questions.

It is clear to us by now that a scientific and intellectual understanding of the problems of Earth and of humankind is not sufficient for *action*. We have known for some time what is happening to Earth, but we have been unable to act on this knowledge, and, as a result, things have become increasingly worse. Some twenty-plus years ago, Maurice Strong organized the United Nations Conference on Environment and Development, where 170 heads of government, leaders of business and civil society, and tens of thousands of others came. Much was discussed and promised and there was much hope, but little seems to have happened.

For this new vision—a new future—a turnaround has to take place. It seems to me that we who have worked on the Earth Charter, who come from different parts of the world, from different cultures, and from different faiths, must set the pace of change starting with ourselves. Gandhi said, "My life is my message." We too, if we are serious about the Earth Charter becoming a reality and a movement, must be able to say, "My life and my actions will be my message."

Therefore, above all, *we* must first learn to live sustainably and make the principles of the Earth Charter part of our lives. If we want people of the global North and of the South to follow the principles and precepts of the Earth Charter, we will have to show by our lives and actions what the Earth Charter is all about. To use Gandhi's words again, "You have to be the change you want others to be." Walking on this road will mean commitment, courage, and fearlessness.

In the last three centuries or so, we have separated the well-being of humans from the well-being of Earth. We need to reconnect and relink the progress of humans with the status of Earth if the healing of Earth and of humans is to take place. The Earth Charter provides a framework for the healing of humans and the healing of Earth.

Adhering to the principles of the Earth Charter will mean that we have to modify our social, economic, and political institutions. For too long we have been at the mercy of those who sell dreams of progress without a whisper of where they are taking us. It is *dharma*, the spirituality of the people, that we must tap if we wish real change and real transformation to take place. Spirituality, however, seems to generate a degree of discomfort in many Western societies, where traditions of objective science separate the secular from the spiritual.

The Earth Charter seeks to combine the threads of scientific, technological, and economic directions with the threads of spirituality, peace, nonviolence, and of the need for compassion for others. The Earth Charter pleads for a new vision, a vision that recognizes that we are all one human family with a common destiny in spite of our different social, cultural, and biological diversity. The Earth Charter will be an important instrument of change, of turning the corner, of a renaissance that will heal Earth and the spirit of humankind. We hope, as the Earth Charter document says in The Way Forward, that "ours [will] be a time remembered for the awakening of a new reverence for life, the firm resolve to achieve sustainability, the quickening of the struggle for justice and peace, and the joyful celebration of life."

Today, with the help of all of you who read this important little volume, we walk firmly along the road to recovery. The artists who have contributed their vision can help provide us with a new path to recognizing the interconnectedness of all humans with Earth. By reading and reflecting on their wisdom, we can begin to heal the fracture and fragment and ruination of our times and bring about wholeness and a return to the sacred. You and I, who are now at the crossroads of history, have a part to play in finding the language and in finding the way inspired by the Earth Charter.

Contributors

Homero Aridjis

As one of Latin America's foremost living literary figures, Homero Aridjis has authored thirty-nine books of poetry and prose. His work has received important literary prizes in Mexico, Italy, France, the United States, and Serbia. He is founder and president of the Group of 100, an environmentalist association of writers, artists, and scientists, and has been honored with the United Nations Environment Program Global 500 Award, the Orion Society's John Hay Award, the Green Cross Millennium Award for International Environmental Leadership, the Natural Resources Defense Council's Force for Nature Award, the Presea Generalisimo José María Morelos, and he has been named Latin Trade magazine's "Environmentalist of the Year." He is a former Mexican Ambassador to Switzerland and the Netherlands, and has been a visiting professor at Indiana University, New York University, and Columbia University. He was President of International PEN, the international writer's organization, 1997–2003, and currently is President Emeritus. He has been an editorial-page columnist since 1994 for the Mexican newspaper *Reforma*. Since April 2007 he has been Mexico's Ambassador to UNESCO.

Rick Bass

Rick Bass is the author of twenty-three books of fiction and nonfiction, including his recent story collection, *The Lives of Rocks*. His first short-story collection, *The Watch*, set in Texas, won the PEN–Nelson Algren Award, and his 2002 collection, *The Hermit's Story*, was a Los Angeles Times Best Book of the Year. Bass's stories have also been awarded the Pushcart Prize and the O. Henry Award and have been collected in *The Best American Short Stories*. Bass lives with his family in northwest Montana's Yaak Valley, where he has been active for more than twenty years in efforts to protect as designated wilderness some of the wildest roadless areas there in "the Land the Wilderness Act Forgot." He is a founding board member of the Yaak Valley Forest Council (www.yaakvalley.org).

Leonardo Boff

Leonardo Boff is one of the founders of liberation theology and was for many years Professor of Systematic and Ecumenical Theology at the Franciscan Institute of Petropolis, Rio de Janeiro. As a result of his book *Church: Charisma and Power* he faced a doctrinal process imposed in 1984 by the Congregation for the Doctrine of Faith in Rome. An "obsequious silence" was imposed on him and he was prohibited from writing and teaching. Later he was a Professor of Ethics and Philosophy of Religion at the State University of Rio de Janeiro. He is the author of more than seventy books in philosophy, theology, spirituality, and ecology. These include, among others, *Jesus Christ Liberator* (1972), *The Maternal Face of God* (1979), *Cry of the Earth, Cry of the Poor* (1998), *Essential Care: An Ethics of Human Nature* (2007), *Global Civilization: Challenges to Society and Christianity* (2005), *World Ethos: A Minimum Consensus among Human Beings* (2002), and *Fundamentalism, Terrorism, and the Future of Humanity* (2006). Currently, he follows grassroots organizations and speaks at conferences and courses on spirituality, ecology, ethics, and ecumenical theology in Brazil and abroad.

Stuart Ching

Stuart Ching is an Associate Professor of English at Loyola Marymount University, Los Angeles. In his fiction and research, he has written about the relationship between the politics of literacy and racial, cultural, and land-based conflicts in Hawai'i and other regions. His stories and essays have appeared in journals such as *North Dakota Quarterly*, *Madison Review*, and *Hawai'i Review*, and in anthologies such as *The Subject Is Story*, *Fractured Feminisms*, *Fourteen Landing Zones*, *The Best of Honolulu Fiction*, *New Voices*, and *Growing Up Local: An Anthology of Poetry and Prose from Hawai'i*.

Kamla Chowdhry

The late Kamla Chowdhry was a protegé of Mahatma Gandhi and a distinguished Gandhian philosopher. She served as an Earth Charter Commissioner and was active in the Earth Charter movement until her death in 2006. She was a Professor at the Indian Institute of Management, Ahmedabad, and a Visiting Professor at Harvard Business School in Cambridge, Massachusetts. She also worked at the Ford Foundation in India as Programme Advisor for Public Planning and Management. She published several papers relating to forestry, environment, sustainable development, and ethics and development. Chowdhry was a founding trustee of the National Foundation for India and was involved in establishing the Institute of Rural Management. She was also a trustee of the Vikram Sarabhai Foundation and Chairperson of the Society for Promotion of Wasteland Development.

Peter Blaze Corcoran

Peter Blaze Corcoran is Professor of Environmental Studies and Environmental Education at Florida Gulf Coast University, where he serves as Director of the Center for Environmental and Sustainability Education. He has been a visiting professor in Australia, The Netherlands, and Fiji. He works extensively in international environmental education with special interest in the South Pacific Island Nations. He is among the founders of the Global Higher Education for Sustainability Partnership and has conducted their consultations with stakeholders in tertiary education in many regions of the world. He is Past President of North American Association for Environmental Education. He serves as Senior Fellow in Education for Sustainability at University Leaders for a Sustainable Future in Washington, D.C., and is Senior Advisor to the Earth Charter Initiative in San José, Costa Rica. His most recent books are *The Earth Charter in Action: Toward a Sustainable World*, published in English, Spanish, and Dutch in The Netherlands by Royal Tropical Institute (KIT) Publishers in 2005, and *Higher Education and the Challenge of Sustainability: Contestation, Critique, Practice, and Promise* with Arjen Wals, published in The Netherlands by Kluwer Academic Press in 2004. He is at work editing, with

Philip Molo Osano, the book *Young People, Education, and Sustainable Development: Exploring Principles, Perspectives, and Praxis* (to be published in 2009).

Alison Hawthorne Deming

Alison Hawthorne Deming is the author of three books of poetry, most recently *Genius Loci* (Penguin, 2005), and three books of nonfiction, including *Writing the Sacred into the Real* (Milkweed, 2001). Her work has earned many awards, including fellowships from the National Endowment for the Arts, the Wallace Stegner Fellowship from Stanford University, the Pablo Neruda Prize, the Bayer Award in Science Writing, and the Walt Whitman Award from the Academy of American Poets. Born in Connecticut, she is a tenth-generation New Englander currently living in Tucson, Arizona, where she is Professor of Creative Writing at the University of Arizona. She renews her connection with the Atlantic North by spending summers on Grand Manan Island in New Brunswick, Canada.

John Lane

A whitewater kayaker and place-based educator, Lane's environmental and outdoor adventure prose has appeared in *Outside, American White Water, Canoe*, and *South Carolina Wildlife*, among many other periodicals. His first collection of personal essays, *Weed Time: Essays from the Edge of a Country Yard* (Briarpatch Press, 1993), described his year living in a cabin near the Great Smoky Mountains. In 1999 the University of Georgia Press published *The Woods Stretched for Miles: Contemporary Southern Nature Writing*, an anthology of southern nature writing Lane coedited with Wofford colleague Gerald Thurmond. His second collection of personal essays, *Waist Deep in Black Water* (2002), appeared from the University of Georgia Press as well. One of the essays in the collection won a Phillip Reed Prize from the Southern Environmental Law Center for the best environmental writing in the South. Georgia also published his book-length personal narrative *Chattooga: Descending into the Myth of Deliverance River* in 2004, and his memoir *Circling Home* followed in 2007. Also a poet and playwright, Lane teaches environmental literature and creative writing at Wofford College and is a founder of the Hub City Writers Project in Spartanburg, South Carolina. His weekly column, "The Kudzu Telegraph," can be found online at www.kudzutelegraph.com.

Robert Michael Pyle

Robert Michael Pyle is the author of fourteen books, including *Walking the High Ridge, Chasing Monarchs, Where Bigfoot Walks, The Thunder Tree,* and *Wintergreen,* which won the John Burroughs Medal for distinguished nature writing. Pyle's latest book, *Skytime in Gray's River: Living for Keeps in a Forgotten Place,* received the 2007 National Outdoor Book Award in natural history and literature. A novel and a collection of poems are in progress. His column, "The Tangled Bank," appeared in fifty-two consecutive issues of *Orion* magazine. A Yale-trained ecologist and a Guggenheim Fellow, he dwells along a tributary of the Lower Columbia River in southwestern Washington State.

Janisse Ray

Writer, naturalist, and activist Janisse Ray is author of three books of literary nonfiction. *Ecology of a Cracker Childhood,* a memoir about growing up on a junkyard in the ruined longleaf pine ecosystem of the Southeast, was published by Milkweed Editions in 1999. The book won a Southeastern Booksellers Award in 1999, an American Book Award in 2000, a Southern Environmental Law Center 2000 Award for Outstanding Writing, and a Southern Book Critics Circle Award in 2000. Ray has published essays and poems in such periodicals as *Audubon, Gray's Sporting Journal, Natural History, Oprah Magazine, Orion, Sierra,* and the *Washington Post.* She is anthologized in *Where We Stand: Voices of Southern Dissent; Elemental South: Earth, Air, Fire, and Water; The Roadless Yaak;* and *The Norton Anthology of Nature Writing.* She holds an MFA from the University of Montana and an honorary doctorate from Unity College. She lectures widely on topics regarding nature, community, sustainability, and the politics of wholeness.

Steven C. Rockefeller

Steven C. Rockefeller is Professor Emeritus of Religion at Middlebury College, Vermont, where he taught for thirty years and served as Dean of the College and Chair of the Religion Department. He received his Master of Divinity from Union Theological Seminary in New York City and his PhD in the philosophy of religion from Columbia University. Among his publications are *John Dewey: Religious Faith and Democratic Humanism* (Columbia, 1991) and *Spirit and Nature: Why the Environment Is a Religious Issue* (Beacon, 1992). He chaired the international Earth Charter drafting committee and presently serves as cochair of the Earth Charter International Council. Active in the field of philanthropy, he chaired the board of the Rockefeller Brothers Fund, an international grant-making foundation, from 1998 to 2006.

Scott Russell Sanders

Born in Tennessee and reared in Ohio, Scott Russell Sanders studied in Rhode Island and Cambridge, England, before going on to become a Distinguished Professor of English at Indiana University. Among his more than twenty books are novels, collections of stories, and works of personal nonfiction, including *Staying Put, Hunting for Hope,* and *A Private History of Awe.* His latest book, forthcoming in 2009, is *A Conservationist Manifesto.* His writing has won the Association of Writers and Writing Programs Creative Nonfiction Award, the John Burroughs Essay Award, and the Lannan Literary Award. He and his wife, Ruth, a biochemist, have reared two children in their hometown of Bloomington, in the hardwood hill country of Indiana's White River Valley.

Lauret Savoy

Lauret Savoy writes across threads of cultural identity to explore their shaping by relationship with and dislocation from the land. A woman of mixed African American, Euro-American, and Native American heritage, and a photographer and professor of geology and environmental studies at Mount Holyoke College, Massachusetts, she coedited *The Colors of Nature: Culture, Identity, and the Natural World* (Milkweed Editions, 2002) with Alison Deming. She edited, with Eldridge and Judy Moores, the anthology *Bedrock: Writers on the Wonders of Geology* (Trinity University Press, 2006, with Barbara Ras). She also coauthored *Living with the Changing California Coast* (with Gary Griggs and Kiki Patsch, University of California Press, 2005).

Chief Jake Swamp

For thirty-seven years, Tekaronianeken (Jake Swamp) has been a Chief of the Mohawk Nation and a representative on the Grand Council of the Haudenosaunee (Iroquois Confederacy). Swamp has worked tirelessly for the communities of the Iroquois people, bridging cultural difference, and addressing environmental and social problems. He has presented the wide range of his experience in indigenous, environmental, and social issues in talks and programs locally and internationally. In 1984 Chief Swamp founded the Tree of Peace Society, a nonprofit organization that builds cross-cultural understanding between Native and non-Native people, promotes environmental and social ethics, and preserves the culture and languages of the Haudenosaunee. Through this work, Swamp has inspired the planting of over 200 million trees. Swamp has appeared in numerous documentaries and television programs. He is the author of the children's book *Giving Thanks, A Native American Good Morning Message* (Lee & Low Books), which is in English and Spanish editions.

Mary Evelyn Tucker

Mary Evelyn Tucker is Senior Lecturer and Research Scholar at Yale University at the School of Forestry and Environmental Studies and the Divinity School. She is codirector with John Grim of the Forum on Religion and Ecology. Together they organized a series of ten conferences on world religions and ecology at the Harvard Center for the Study of World Religions. They are series editors for the ten volumes from the conferences. She is also Research Associate at the Harvard Yenching Institute and at the Reischauer Institute of Japanese Studies at Harvard. She is the author of *Worldly Wonder: Religions Enter Their Ecological Phase* (Open Court Press, 2003), *Moral and Spiritual Cultivation in Japanese Neo-Confucianism* (SUNY, 1989), and *The Philosophy of Qi* (Columbia

University Press, 2007). She coedited *Worldviews and Ecology* (Orbis, 1994), *Buddhism and Ecology* (Harvard, 1997), *Confucianism and Ecology* (Harvard, 1998), and *Hinduism and Ecology* (Harvard, 2000) and edited Thomas Berry's *Evening Thoughts* (Sierra Club, 2007). She is a member of the Interfaith Partnership for the Environment at the United Nations Environment Programme (UNEP). She served as a member of the International Earth Charter Drafting Committee and is currently a member of the Earth Charter International Council.

Terry Tempest Williams

The work of celebrated nature writer and activist Terry Tempest Williams has been widely anthologized in many national and international publications. Williams is perhaps best known for her book *Refuge: An Unnatural History of Family and Place* (Pantheon, 1991), now regarded as a classic in American nature writing. She is also the author of *The Open Space of Democracy* (Orion, 2004), which offers a sharp-edged perspective on the ethics of politics and place, the soul of democracy and the responsibilities of citizen participation. Her latest book, *Mosaic: Finding Beauty in a Broken World* (Pantheon, 2008), provides a glimpse into the fragmented emotional landscape of postwar Rwanda. Williams has been a fellow for the John Simon Guggenheim Memorial Foundation and received a Lannan Literary Fellowship in Creative Nonfiction. She is currently on the advisory board of the National Parks and Conservation Association, the Nature Conservancy, and the Southern Utah Wilderness Alliance. Williams has testified before the United States Congress twice regarding women's health and the environmental links associated with cancer and has been a strong advocate for America's Redrock Wilderness Act. She has been inducted into the Rachel Carson Honor Roll and has received the National Wildlife Federation's Conservation Award for Special Achievement. Formerly Naturalist-in-Residence at the Utah Museum of Natural History, Williams lives in Moose, Wyoming.

A. James Wohlpart

Jim Wohlpart is Professor of English at Florida Gulf Coast University, where he serves as the Associate Dean of the College of Arts and Sciences and the Associate Director of the Center for Environmental and Sustainability Education. In addition, he is a Redesign Scholar with the National Center for Academic Transformation and is on the Advisory Board of the University Press of Florida. Holding a PhD and a BA from the University of Tennessee and an MA from Colorado State University, Wohlpart pursues scholarship on American Indian literature, women's literature, and environmental literature. He has published essays on Emily Dickinson, Walt Whitman, Nathaniel Hawthorne, Frederick Douglass, and other American writers. He is currently working on a book of literary analysis and creative nonfiction tentatively titled *A Mind of Sky and Thunder: Remembering the Forgotten Language.*